BORN TO LEARN

—

*Real World Learning Through
Unschooling and Immersion*

Kytka Hilmar-Jezek

A Distinct Press Book
2015

Born To Learn
Real World Learning Through Unschooling and Immersion

SECOND EDITION

This is the SECOND EDITION.

Please note that the first edition had only 80 printed pages and had a word count
under 20,000. This second edition has 234 printed pages and a word count of over
50,000.

Summary: Don't waste your time homeschooling or attending public school when
learning is all around you in each and every experience, each and every day. Children
are learning all of the time. In fact, we all are.

1. Education & Reference: Unschooling 2. Teacher Resources: Homeschooling 3.
Parent Participation

Library of Congress Cataloging-in-Publication Data
2015909806

Hilmar-Jezek, Kytka 1964-
Born To Learn: Real World Learning Through Unschooling and Immersion

ISBN-10:1943103003
ISBN-13:978-1-943103-00-3

Printed in the U.S.A.
10 9 8 7 6 5 4 3 2 1

Table of Contents

I

WELCOME

Hello and welcome. My name is Kytka and I wanted to thank you for choosing to spend this time with me today. This book is an introduction to new paradigm ideas on education in a rapidly changing world.

This book is primarily a transcribed tele summit interview which I did on the subject of how children learn, especially without the interference of and formal schooling. I've been told that the information herein is so valuable and it was requested numerous times, so I chose to have the transcription available for those who expressed an interest.

I first published the direct transcription without chapters, pages, anything, but I then realized that there was a strong need for this information so I have created this second edition which I hope will provide a more enjoyable reading experience for you and will help to guide you in choosing what you feel is best for your child.

Please keep in mind when reading this that it was a transcribed interview. Sometimes when we speak and all of our natural passion just flows, we may sound condescending or judgmental but that is never the intent. (Okay, sometimes when 'I' speak, it may sound that way) I simply ask you to remember that the intention is to share MY experience and how it has been of benefit to me. I understand that your experience and circumstance may be very different, and I respect that and you for the choices you have made.

In my own family I am one of two girls. I have a sister and we are like night and day. I am the radical home and unschooler, and my sister is the deeply committed public school teacher. While we walk entirely different paths in life, we both have a deep love of children and how they learn and we can respect one another's different paths and choices.

This is not solely about education. While it is discussed, the true root of this interview (come book) is on the subject of how children learn. But first, let's take a quick look at the definitions...

education, noun

: the action or process of teaching someone especially in a school, college, or university
: the knowledge, skill, and understanding that you get from attending a school, college, or university
: a field of study that deals with the methods and problems of teaching

learning, noun

: the activity or process of gaining knowledge or skill by studying, practicing or experiencing something
: knowledge or skill gained from learning
: the act or experience of one that learns
: modification of a behavioral tendency by experience (as exposure to conditioning)

The way I see it is that education is something that is given to you, like water poured into a vase. Whereas learning is something that you discover and become on your own, you are the vase. Education is so backward. We don't teach children to cultivate their intelligence through critical thought and doubt, rather, we teach them to memorize and accept established ideas, beliefs and discoveries without questioning anything, in order to make our society continue to run smoothly.

The knowledge we should be encouraging is discernment not information. Unfortunately, it is not 'intelligence' our current education system is striving towards, it's 'intellectuality', or in other words, who can memorize the most. This is measured by testing and every year there seem to be more and more tests and therefore, more and more opportunities to feel like a failure.

According to unschooling pioneer John Holt, "...the anxiety children feel at constantly being tested, their fear of failure, punishment, and disgrace, severely reduces their ability both to perceive and to remember, and drives them away from the material being studied into strategies for fooling teachers into thinking they know what they really don't know."

The content within these pages is radical. It is against the status quo. We should strive to be living examples of living a fulfilled life. We should motivate them to understand how their minds and bodies work so that each one can find their own path to knowledge.

I believe that we should be teaching children how to be more fully human. You may note that sometimes I seem to go off topic, such as describing infant behavior and the way children play, and so forth. I do this because it all ties together in how children ultimately learn, perceive and interact with the world around them.

We need to raise humans and not people who are ready, straight off the assembly line, to work by their early twenties and even earlier. But sadly, this is precisely what the school machine does. Stifling their creativity, silencing their voice, teaching them to follow and consume. School is a place of social hierarchies where pressure to perform dominates the day.

> *"Education is a method whereby one acquires a higher grade of prejudices."*
>
> *- Laurence J. Peterlea*

Our children are taught to anxiously compete with each other to find out who has a better short term memory. They are stripped of their freedoms to explore and connect with the natural rhythms of life around them. They are disconnected from nature. They are tested and labeled and made to fit into a one size fits all box.

But human beings are not 'one size fits all'.

That is why I believe that school is a training ground and convenient system for robot like machines, not human beings. A place for education, but not for any true learning.

"Education is a state-controlled manufactory of echoes."
- Norman Douglas

II

INTRODUCTION

I am the mother of three wonderful children. I am blessed to have Zachary who is 22, Zanna who is 17 and Zynnia who is 14 as my children. They were all unschooled. They all have on line businesses. They are all entrepreneurs who have experienced living in and traveling to several different countries. They have attended numerous personal development and educational seminars. They have taught workshops, created products and are creating multiple income streams which will secure their futures. They may be young, but they are teaching adults how they do it.

If the world as we know it stopped and just "turned off", they all have the skills to survive. They know how to build shelter, find and prepare food, plant seed, knit or sew, trade and barter.

From living in a shack with a dirt floor in a third world country, to living at a luxury estate of dear entrepreneurial friends, they have the ability to fit in and converse from those uneducated to those ultra-educated. My personal thought is that it is because they have been exposed to so much in life, at completely opposite ends of the spectrum, so they have an insight that many people do not have the opportunity to have.

It may also be how they have learned...

They never received a "traditional education" and instead were raised on Rudolf Steiner's Waldorf Pedagogy principles while homeschooling, through complete immersion, apprenticeships and a free range or 'hack' learning. While they did follow a strict curriculum for the first year or two, each year I relaxed more and more because I had the ability to see what worked and what didn't work. I was able to measure their advancement by their interest and their passion for subjects.

All three of my children were born at home and parented in what is called the 'attachment parenting' style. Growing more main stream with each passing year, I confess that it was hard to stay true to my heart when they were young. Support was nowhere to be found and if it came, it was usually in the form of yahoo discussion lists with other "radical mamas". In the last 90's I was active on numerous discussion groups and forums and was hailed for my honest and "in your face" views. I was called a pioneer and a living example of what the future might bring. We were giving birth to and raising 'the new children'. Many came to call them 'Indigos'.

A wonderful human being and a personal mentor, Joseph Chilton Pearce, author of such classics such as *Magical Child, The Crack In The Cosmic Egg, The Biology of Transcendence: A Blueprint of the Human Spirit, The Heart-Mind Matrix: How the Heart Can Teach the Mind New Ways to Think* and numerous other award winning and bestselling books wrote the following about me:

> *"That a single individual could accomplish so much as Kytka Hilmar-Jezek has, while at the same time tending to her family is an admirable example to us all, both parents and all citizens interested in improving the quality of our populations' intelligence and character. In no way can the importance of her work be over-emphasized. Dear Kytka, needless to say, I find your work extremely important and your efforts quite admirable. I surely wish you all the best.*
>
> *- Sincerely Yours, Joseph Chilton Pearce."*

I share this here because my views have always been "out of the box" and challenging to the norm. I have never written (or lived) what would be the status quo. Instead, I have always spoken of things that matter deeply to the movement of family, parenting, education and life in the future in a challenging and radical way. Yet the way I share what in my experience has been true is usually unsettling to people. This is because it's not the "norm". It makes people uncomfortable and uneasy because it is unfamiliar and different.

Since I began to put myself out as a voice for a different way of looking at these things, I have been attacked for not being more delicate about the subject matter. I have been told I can be offensive, condescending, judgmental and acrid. People often react with shock because I touch deeply on subjects that we all hold too close to home and change can be frightening.

> *"Frightened of change? But what can exist without it? What's closer to nature's heart? Can you take a hot bath and leave the firewood as it was? Eat food without transforming it? Can any vital process take place without something being changed? Can't you see? It's just the same with you – and just as vital to nature."*
>
> *- Marcus Aurelius*

What I discuss in this book requires you to have an open mind. To allow yourself to imagine a new paradigm. To step out of the comfort of the box. To be open to change…

I remember when I was a childbirth educator and I held classes in my home on having a safe home birth. I would normally get five or six couples to sign up for the classes and the majority of them wanted support on their home birth decision and journey. Interestingly enough, there would always be the one couple that wanted to fight against any facts I presented on home birth, arguing the entire time that their doctor knew better.

Why were they in the class? I would always close these arguments with the suggestion that they should then attend childbirth classes with their doctor, or at the hospital where they were planning to give birth. After all, mine was a class aimed specifically at home birthing parents.

What fascinated me was that each class had such a couple. I spoke to my midwife friend who had been in the profession for over forty years. She said something to me that I will never forget. "Kytka, please do not put any more thought and energy into this. The answer is so simple, and yet, sometimes these are the hardest things to face in life. *For them to 'agree' with what you present in your class, something in their mind first has to first accept that what they have been told, have been taught (all these years) is wrong. In other words, they have been told a lie.* Who lied to them? Perhaps their own Doctor, perhaps their own parents - that is not for you to solve."

It was so simple, and yet it made absolute sense. She was right.

To allow the opening for a new reality, you must be willing to question the current reality and questioning one's reality can be earth shattering for some. How could I have missed it?

"Here's To The Crazy Ones. The misfits. The rebels. The trouble-makers. The round pegs in the square holes. The ones who see things differently. They're not fond of rules, and they have no respect for the status-quo. You can quote them, disagree with them, glorify, or vilify them. About the only thing you can't do is ignore them. Because they change things. They push the human race forward. And while some may see them as the crazy ones, we see genius. Because the people who are crazy enough to think they can change the world - are the ones who DO!"

- Slogan for Apple Computers, Steve Jobs

I did not know then that my entire life would be experiencing things that feel common sense, practical and logical to me in a way where people both admire the results of my parenting, and yet at the same time, often attack me for being so different because to understand me and my reality means they will have to question their own. It places me in a strange position and has been a dilemma in my life, a challenge that I constantly have to work with.

So yes, my children were born at home, before it was popular. They were carried in a sling when mothers were running alongside with jogging strollers. They were raised on a 100% raw and living goods diet, which now is gaining popularity, but was almost unheard of then. They were home schooled and then unschooled, immersing themselves in subjects and hacking it along the way. They grew up with no television, no Nintendo or Atari (or X-Box), no Disney World. There were no baseball games and I surely was not a soccer mom. There were no birthday parties at Chuck-e-Cheese's and McDonald's with friends during sleepovers. There were no sleepovers. They weren't told to color in the lines of their coloring books because they had no coloring books, until they made their own.

Yet they loved to read, to play games, to discover new things and to challenge their friends to do and be more. People often worry about socialization with homeschoolers, but I think that is focusing on the wrong challenge. The problem is not will they be social, the truer question is will they be able to relate to children their own age?

My children grew up surrounded by people of all ages, young and old. They could care for a newborn and knew how to hold and handle him and they would do their best to make an elderly person comfortable. They were comfortable speaking with adults and with children. But I have to admit, they did not much enjoy conversations with typically schooled children their own age.

They found them to be boring. They did not care who was wearing what shoes and what new video game came out. They did not like gossip about so and so and didn't want to be a part of talking bad about someone. If the child began to talk about why they don't play with this person or that person, my children became very uncomfortable and even angry.

"Why do they not respect this person?" "Why do they put

that person aside just because he does not have the right back-pack?" I would always shrug my shoulders and answer "I do not know…." Allowing them to make their own conclusions and find their own way, using their own inner compass.

They disliked that so much of the conversation had to do with materialistic pursuits (*I have a new this, I have a new that, did you see the new this, did you see the new that, I want the new this, I want the new that….*) It seemed it was always about something outside of themselves and my children were frustrated that they just could not have a *real* conversation with any children their own age. But I had three of them, so they became best friends with each other and to this day, people cannot believe the closeness of relationship they share. "You mean they are sisters and they don't hate each other?"

Yes. That is exactly what I mean. Where in this time or space is it written that siblings are supposed to hate each other? That they are supposed to hate their parents and other family members for that matter? I am happy I missed the memo and that our family respects, honors and loves the fact that for whatever reason, we were placed on this journey together. It is a subject of pride and one we practice gratitude over.

All of my friends bought their children everything of the latest and greatest goodies and gadgets and then would try to pass things along to me for my children. Not casually, but almost with a desperation, as if I NEEDED to have these things (strollers, cribs, bikes, Barbie dolls, Hot Wheels), but my rules were strict. I wanted my children's toys to be all natural and to awaken the imagination. They could make their own toys. They could take a stone and turn it into a marble or a little chair for one of their tiny woodland fairies. They could take a stick and use it to build a teepee or as a sword to fight the imaginary dragon. I wanted their play to be alive in their minds, and to take place in nature. I wanted them to experience discovery and adventure and to look for clues of life and death, calm and storm all around them.

I also followed Rudolf Steiner's signs for readiness that he taught to Waldorf School teachers. Steiner taught that in the realm of the physical, a child's limbs should be in proportion with the body and head and that this is a sign of school readiness. Baby fat should be all gone and there should be greater definition in the face. Emotionally, the young child who once expressed strong emotions through sudden outbursts now has feelings that begin to deepen. A child can actually talk about feelings being hurt and being sad. Socially, the school ready child begins to form deeper friendships, ones in which the child feels an affinity or loyalty to certain people and will express the desire to be with them. In their mind, a child is ready when he can find certain memories and recall them at will. This is different than the memory of a three or four year old. A younger child's memory is triggered by a smell, sight, or rhythmic verse. When the memory is "freed" around age six or seven, the child can just think and find the memory, no trigger is needed. The brain has developed to do this at this time.

At UCLA's School of Education, Richard Cohen studies how children learn. He has found that "along with memory, children begin to develop a capacity to understand symbolic concepts." He concluded that "kids learn through their experiences. They're not able to sit back and think symbolically, the way we like to think most of us are able to do. So most children under the age of 6 or 7 learn best by handling and manipulating real objects, and experiencing real things. They need to explore their world for a long time before they can begin to attach symbols or concepts to things."

Older children also access imagination, which is very different than fantasy. Fantasy play requires props to make the fantasy alive whereas for imagination, no physical objects are needed. The child can see and experience the play in his mind. He can be happy just to sit and play with vision in his heads. Children that have made this shift also recognize mathematics and the language arts. They love to play with words, make rhymes or change words in songs and verses.

Kytka Hilmar-Jezek

In an article entitled *Education for Creative Thinking: The Waldorf Approach*, author Joan Almon relates a story from the childhood of the well-known Viennese kindergarten teacher Bronja Zahlingen: "As a child, she loved to play with small objects on a deep window seat in her bedroom. She would create a scene with little dolls and houses and play with them for long periods of time. She remembers that one day, when she was about six years old, she set up a scene as usual but then closed her eyes and played 'inside'. Imagination had been born, and she was able to participate in her play in a new way."

Ms. Almon uses this story to point up the essential reason why the academic subjects must wait for the development of this inner imagination, and why imagination should be a central pillar of the first grade curriculum:

"The development of imagination is an essential step in thinking, but where the development of fantasy has been curtailed, the development of imagination also suffers. Without imagination, one cannot picture an event in history, a verbal problem in mathematics, or the characters of a book. To approach academic subjects without imagination is a dull affair at best, and it is not surprising that children who are being educated without benefit of imagination at the elementary level find learning so uninteresting. Their newborn imagination is not being fed and nourished. Those who have been asked to master academics at the kindergarten level may suffer an even deeper problem, for in them imagination may be aborted before being born. There are indications that children who learn to read before age six or seven lose their early advantages, for they lose interest in reading and may eventually suffer burnout. This is not surprising when one thinks of how dull reading and learning are without the benefit of imagination to bring them alive. In contrast, in my experience, the children who are the best players in the kindergarten and have the most active fantasy tend to become the most imaginative elementary pupils with the greatest interest in reading. They also tend to be the best-adjusted emotionally, both as children and even as adolescents and adults."

When I studied all of this and did the research, it just made sense to me. I felt that children were being pushed to grow up too fast.

In *Ten Ways to Destroy the Imagination of Your Child* by Mr. Anthony Esolen, he writes: "Play dates, soccer practice, day care, political correctness, drudgery without facts, television, video games, constant supervision, endless distractions: these and other insidious trends in child rearing and education are now the hallmarks of childhood. Almost everything we are doing to children now constricts their imaginations, usually to serve the ulterior motives of the constrictors."

So we sent them to school, just to make it easier on ourselves? In the process, we strip them of their imaginations and of their freedom. We break their will and make them submit to the masters. Then we all gather together and pay ourselves on the back and say it is a good thing, all in the name of education.

Children need to be schooled. Otherwise they will not amount to anything except cute little imbeciles. Is that what we really believe? We don't. So why then do we keep sending them to school?

> "*What you know you can't explain, but you feel it. You've felt it your entire life, that there's something wrong with the world. You don't know what it is, but it is there, like a splinter in your mind, driving you mad.*"
>
> *- Morpheus "The Matrix"*

Rudolf Steiner spoke of "*The Kingdom of Childhood*" and described it in a way that it was a sacred place, and I wanted to honor my children by allowing them to remain there as long as they wanted (and needed).

When Steiner lectured about childhood, he would stress the tremendous importance of doing everything with the knowledge that children are citizens of both the spiritual and the earthly worlds. He warned of the dangers of stressing the intellect too early. He proposed a teaching that was concrete and pictorial based on the children's needs. He believed that the spiritual also needed to be addressed, the education of children's souls through wonder and reverence. And he stressed the importance of first presenting the "whole," and then the parts, to awaken and ignite the children's imagination. For he believed that from their imagination would come great things for their futures, and the future of our planet and species.

Because of this, I did not rush into anything. All in due time. I wanted them to enjoy fantasy play and to awaken their imaginations in a gentle and unforced way.

"Mama, when can I get a bicycle?" Zachary asked.

My answer came. "When you master riding your tricycle."

And so it was.

My children were unfolding naturally and the world would unfold around them in a slow and rhythmic manner. They walked the world in wonder and looked forward to milestones and successes.

I had allowed them to grow in the kingdom of childhood and I fought every day to protect that kingdom because society stood against me. I created a cocoon of a world where they were left to explore their own imaginations and much time was spent in silence.

"The child's language is melodious. The words hide and protect themselves in the melody – the words that have come shyly out of the silence. They almost disappear again in the silence. There is more melody than content in the words of the child. It is as though silence were accumulating within the child as a reserve for the adult, for the noisy world of the child's later years as an adult. The adult who has preserved within himself not only something of the language of childhood but also something of its silence, too, has the power to make others happy."

- *Max Picard, The World of Silence, 1952*

Silence too, can be magical and golden, as they say. In a world so noisy, it is a healing gift.

"Proper education and proper teaching," writes Max Picard, "are based on the substance of silence."

For silence, is not an absence, but a presnce. It is noise, rather, that is the absence, both of the significant word and of the fullness of being that silence allows us to hear. Silence belongs to man as the creature who possesses the word; noise, to the creature whom words possess, lashing him on, on, mechanically, without rest, without meaning.

My children flourished in this place, and they trusted that I would provide the tools they needed at each new phase of their development. They were busy in their work of play and they felt they earned each next phase, and when they got there, whatever it was (*bicycle, roller skates, and power tools*) was then even more valued and enjoyed. Being given the gift of life has been enveloped in gratitude, appreciation and joy.

> *"I sometimes wake in the early morning & listen to the soft breathing of my child & I think to myself, this is one thing I will never regret & I carry that quiet with me all day long."*

> *- Brian Andreas*

My friends' children, on the other hand, by the time they were 5 or 6 they had a trike, a bike and a scooter. They had several pets who all lived and died (of neglect and mishandling) and had the attitude that they have "been there and done that". Always looking to "one up" the last thing they got or experienced, they grew bored easily and had little or no respect for their things (living or otherwise).

I did not see a peace and calm in them. I did not see a reverence for their things. I did not see patience. I did not see respect. I did not see wonder. Instead they appeared bored, spoiled, unimpressed and even cynical. Yet they were children. It made me sad and my own children did not like to play with them. "All they want to do is play those dumb video games", "they don't want to go outside, and they said it is too hot", "he said his mom told him he is not allowed to get dirty", "she does not know how to climb a tree", "she said my fort was stupid and just a few rags hung from ropes"...

These children were impatient and would not hold their attention to anything for long. Easily frustrated and bored, they never really mastered anything except whining that they wanted the next thing. It frustrated my children and agitated me. (*I could write an entire book on whining and how this is NOT a natural form of communication!*)

Twenty years later I have seen these children go to juvenile detention, jail, down the path of drugs and addiction and to the hospital, Baker-acted. I even experienced some tragedy. A dear friend lost her son at the age of 17. He committed suicide. Such a beautiful life waiting to be lived out and for whatever reason, he did not see it.

Where is the gratitude, appreciation and joy in these children's lives? After all, to the naked eye it looks like they have it all. It is my children who were somehow held back or neglected in terms of all the latest trends. They are the ones who have gone without...

> *"Don't handicap your children by making their lives easy."*
>
> *- Robert A. Heinlein*

Maybe the more we have, the less we see the value of any of it. My own beliefs on parenting are strong. I think too many people spoil their children giving them what they did not have as children. This is not a solution, but a big problem. I think whining should be for dogs who crouch by the door, needing to be let out and not for children, or worse yet, their parents who respond in the same tones. I think most of today's children have been given so much since birth, that they have a sense of entitlement that makes them vain, insensitive and apathetic. They have little interest or concern in anything but their own wants and needs and I shudder to think what kind of adults these children will become.

I have to warn you, this material primarily comes from a passionate discussion I had on an unschooling tele-summit which was transcribed and I did not want to have anyone else edit it. I have this way of "in your face" talking that pushes some away and some people really do not like me because of it. But I am not interested in a popularity contest.

I have gone through incredible difficulty on my own life journey and even in the midst of the greatest adversity; I still managed to keep my priorities straight in terms of my parenting. I made sacrifices and most times, took the harder path and not the path of least resistance. Parenting requires dedication, commitment and sacrifice and I modeled my own style after tribal communities and primitive societies which honor natural cycles, understand growth and honor children. This meant that work was secondary and my social life was secondary.

I dedicated my life to being their guard and guardian. I missed many things, but I made that choice. I did not want to miss their growing up. And it is that simple. We choose the kind of parent we want to be. Those that say they cannot because of this reason or that reason are making excuses and when you make an excuse, then that is your choice. You choose the excuse.

This book is about my experience and my choice. I did not write it to try to convince you or stand on a soap box shouting that my way is better than your way. I only know that my way is what works for me. It is the way I constructed for my family based on what I discovered and wanted and learned along the way. I can speak from a place of strength in knowing what I know and what works for me. But this does not mean that it will work for you, and I do not suggest that this is for everyone...

During the care and raising of my own children I continued my studies and I became a Doctor of Naturopathy and a Certified Advanced Master of Neuro-Lingusistic Programming, also known as NLP.

It was important to me to instill a love of learning in each of them and so I had to model this activity myself. Of course, I do love learning and as a result, I also carry Certifications in Clinical Hypnotherapy, Psychotherapy, Complete Mind Therapy, Hypnotic Pain Control, Noesitherapy, Rapid Results Consulting and I am a Certified Practitioner of Time Empowerment.

In addition, I have also completed the requirements and my studies as a Minister, Certified Childbirth Educator, Labor Assistant, Reiki Master, Mayan Shaman, Soul Counselor as well as a Doctor of Philosophy in Religion and Spiritual Studies.

But wait... there's more! I have attended over $250,000 worth of personal empowerment seminars, workshops, conferences and intensives as well as read over 25,000 books on my journey.

Wow... why would anyone do all of that and still be 100% committed to being a full time parent who works from home?

I am not sharing this with you to impress you in any way, but rather to impress upon you that I have spent the majority of my entire adult life in study and on the quest for of information. I repeat, I wanted my children to have a lifelong love of learning, and so I modeled that for them.

For me, life IS learning. It has served me well and made my journey an enjoyable one. I wanted to gift this to my own children, so this was the choice I made. Was it hard at times? You bet! I had to stay up late, cancel things, shift things around, juggle a bit and so on, but they needed to see how you do not make excuses and rather push through looking for solutions. We never had 'problems', we had 'challenges' and my children learned that challenges are like putting together a puzzle. You just keep tying until you finish. I was tenacious and resolved to keep going until the puzzle was finished. Now these are characteristics I see and admire in my own children. They don't quit. They push through and nothing is seen as impossible.

Nothing is impossible, the word itself says 'I'm possible'!

- Audrey Hepburn

In retrospect, I can humbly confess that I accomplished all of the above because I was constantly trying to somehow *prove* that I was on the right path as a parent. My powerful inner guide was not enough.

Seeing how they literally blossomed and grew - healthy, happy and loved and welcomed by everyone - that was not enough. I wanted society to speed up and match what I had experienced, tested and proven in the science lab of my own life. I wanted culture to catch up with me. I wanted not to be a pioneer - but to just be accepted as a fellow parent on the journey to do the best I could by my children.

When I look at the list of my accomplishment now it is almost ridiculous to me and oddly enough, though I use all of the learnings in everyday life, I am not actively professionally practicing any of them. Life is simply too short and there is too much to be enjoyed that I cannot sit in one place and imagine myself doing only one thing. My life has been structured in a way that it is an adventure and this is true for my children's lives as well.

The proof is in the pudding.

Everywhere I go, my children come with me. (Well, now Zachary does not. He is 22 and has moved away from home and is happily enjoying his own life.)At events, conferences and meetings, people come up to me and discuss how they have never met children like mine. I get comments like "you should be so proud".

I move away from that. Accepting a sense of pride would mean that I somehow trained them up to perform in a way that is likable by the crowd.

No. I cannot take credit because I did not really do that much.

I simply stepped out of the way and maintained my courage

and my position in the face of constant disagreement, voiced opinion and attack. I held true and I stood my ground. I maintained my convictions and my commitment to allowing them to live in the kingdom of childhood. I protected them from outside influence and allowed their imaginations to soar. I instilled a lifelong love of learning in them and I shared my passion for reading. I allowed them to choose what they wanted to study and I provided the resources for them to delve in, unguided and undisturbed for however long they needed to gather what they believed to be enough understanding to satisfy their own personal drive.

I remained strong - and if you take anything away from my sharing here - it is that you need to be strong too, for your child. Trust yourself, and while it may not be the popular choice, the normal choice or the choice that everyone else is choosing - trust that *you know best* and make the best choices for yourself and your child.

Yes, my long list of titles, accomplishments and certifications above is quite long and expansive in its subject matter but as I made the journey, I was simply trying to find the best answers that worked for me and made sense to my parenting style. While it was, at times, a difficult path then, the journey has put me into a very unique circle of people now. I am blessed to experience intimate discussions with some of the world's most incredible leaders and luminaries and continue to be blessed to be in the presence of so many of my mentors who I can now also proudly call my friends, and all this with my children at my side.

My primary interest at this stage of my life is to share the things I have experienced and learned along my journey with other parents who may be on a similar path or who wish to understand more about the alternatives to mainstream that are available. To share what a life living away from the mainstream or cultural norm may look like. For this reason, I have created over a hundred websites over the years where I have shared the different steps along our family journey.

Writing is my outlet and my passion so I have also authored several books, some under my own name and others under pen names. My primary "job" is as a publisher and I help others to share their messages and unique journeys. Of course my work has to do with books, where else can we get such wonderful information for learning?

I now travel extensively with my daughters and do a lot of speaking, training, coaching and consulting. I have used my creative entrepreneurial skills and background to marry my work with my passion and I consciously model this for my children so that they too may have a life filled with the passions they have and experience the adventures they want.

My goal has always been to inspire in them an ongoing love of learning. To awaken a feeling where their work is their passion, so that they never feel burdened or trapped by meeting their material needs, but instead thrive and experience wealth doing what they love while making a positive contribution to the world. To me that is the truest definition of success.

> Do what you love and you will never have to work a day in your life.

So again I wish to remind you, the information I share is often radical in nature and what most would call 'out of the box'.

It is not in any way traditional or mainstream.

I touch deeply on personal subjects where people have deep feelings based on beliefs and values and for whatever reason (*I think it is Gods sense of humor*) I do not have the proper vocabulary or diplomacy skills to not piss you off...

So, if at any time you feel triggered by something I may be sharing, I ask that you set judgment aside for a moment, take a deep breath and just continue to read.

> *"When you grow up you tend to get told the world is the way it is and your life is just to live your life inside the world. Try not*

to bash into the walls too much. Try to have a nice family life, have fun, save a little money. That's a very limited life. Life can be much broader once you discover one simple fact, and that is - everything around you that you call life, was made up by people that were no smarter than you. And you can change it, you can influence it, you can build your own things that other people can use. The minute that you understand that you can poke life and actually something will, you know if you push in, something will pop out the other side, that you can change it, you can mold it. That's maybe the most important thing. It's to shake off this erroneous notion that life is there and you're just gonna live in it, versus embrace it, change it, improve it, make your mark upon it. I think that's very important and however you learn that, once you learn it, you'll want to change life and make it better, cause it's kind of messed up, in a lot of ways. Once you learn that, you'll never be the same again."

- Steve Jobs, PBS 'One Last Thing' documentary, 1994

My information is based on my own life experience. It is my hope that it will introduce a different way of thinking, feeling and being. That it will show an alternative way. I understand it is not for everyone nor do I want everyone to be the same or be on the same path.

However, if you found your way here today, something inside of you may wanted to hear it, so all I ask is that you suspend those beliefs and judgments for the duration of this read.

Open your mind to the possibility of *'what if'* and remember, you can only be inspired by one or two ideas and don't have to take on the whole package.

Let's begin...

1

THE EASY WAY

"A man only learns in two ways, one by reading, and the other by association with smarter people."
- Will Rogers

The true objective of education is to inspire and it is to prepare the young to educate themselves throughout their lives. Home and unschooled children are entrusted to find their own learning become creators, leaders and the game changers of society.

I cannot clearly define homeschooling here because there are so many ways people define it themselves. Some parents follow a strict curriculum, others are much freer in how they plan their children's learning. For the sake of this work, I am focusing primarily on unschooling. I define unschooling as not having a strict guideline or curriculum which one must follow. I define it as allowing the child choose what he wants to know about and then providing the resources and the opportunity of complete immersion to learn all he can about the specific subject.

Does math or English or social studies lag behind when this happens? Yes. But it allows the child to quickly recognize his own strengths and interests. If my son wanted to build a pyramid, he would have to know mathematics and physics to an advance degree. I believe that if the desire to build the pyramid was that great, then during the period of immersion, he would master the mathematics and physics necessary to construct a pyramid. (*And I am imagining the ones in Egypt and not a simple cardboard cutout on the table*).

I believe in the human will and in the fire of desire to accomplish what we want when we are allowed to do so, especially when supported in the task. Unschooling then, in my opinion, allows for this to take place. Many of the world's greatest geniuses all had in common that they were pulled from the school environment. They were freed to discover the undiscovered. They had the imagination to '*see*' a different way and the drive to try to build what they had seen.

I believe unschooled children can accomplish great things in the world because they feel valuable, innovative, and creative. They inherently know that have something of intrinsic value to contribute. They have something that is not learned but rather formed from their own will, so it is uniquely their own.

Schooling, on the other hand, is the imposition of intellectual content and facts upon the child. It is the filling of them with our outside information, burying them in all of our research, entering all of our data. Children are not data banks....

> *"Children aren't coloring books. You don't get to fill them with your favorite colors."*
> - *Khaled Hosseini*

Learning is ongoing, spontaneous and relevant to the surroundings and the situation one is in at the current moment. Learning should be an exciting and engaging voyage of discovery of the world, and of oneself.

So the primary difference I see is that unschooling is an invitation to awaken and ennoble capabilities that exist within the child. Where traditional schooling is to fill the child with facts that we, as a collective have decided upon. Self-learning gives opportunity for new and untapped discovery whereas traditional learning is a regurgitation of already established discovery.

If you look at it in this way, you can conclude that by deciding to fill the child with what we know, and taking up that space (imagining that a child is like a container) then we actually take away the space necessary for the child's own discovery.

What if your child had the capabilities of Einstein within? How would you know? Do children that become filled with greatness come with a special tag that gives instructions on how to rear that child? I don't think so.

So how do you know that your child is not the one? What if he is and you send this child to school. He has no choice. Maybe he told you "I hate school" or "I am bored at school" but you ignored it because culture and society has already made us believe that all kids say this...

So your child has to perform at school for 8-10 hours per day and then his time is filled with satisfying social obligations after school (soccer, baseball, sleepovers). When does your child have time to become Einstein? Do you think that in high school, in the science lab, he will have a spontaneous moment where he stands at the chalkboard and suddenly writes $E = mc2$? That is not how is happens.

What is needed is time to imagine and explore. Time to take the journey in the mind and then try to replicate it in the real world. To ask the necessary questions and overcome the logical obstacles. To see it in the mind so clearly that one almost obsessed with making it real and tangible. So much so that they are driven with the strongest will and passion to make it real.

When do children today have this luxury of time? And with all of the distractions, do they just sit and imagine or sit and think? Not usually. They sit and play a video game. Or they sit and watch a movie. Or they sit and chat with their buddies on Facebook. Wherever they go, they are disturbed by radio, television, iPads and phones. There is no quiet time to imagine, to think or to reflect.

And besides, they have somewhere they need to be every day for the next eighteen years and that is school. School will get them the learning they need to get by. Why think at all? It's easier to play the video game and be immersed in someone else's imagination, right?

But back to the difference between unschooling and what we know as traditional schooling. And what a profound difference it is...

In one way we see that child as this container that is assumed to be empty - where the objective is to fill it. The other way is where see the child as a container that is assumed to be full - where the objective is to draw from deep within.

That difference is significant and we need to understand how we view our child, because education and parenting decisions will be made on this view. Much like the optimist sees the glass as half full and the pessimist sees it as half empty – take a moment to really ask yourself and think about how you see your child.

> Does your child need to be filled, or is your child already full and we just need to draw and pull forth from the child?

This may seem a simple exercise, but if you really go deep into this belief you will see that many of your parenting decisions you are making come down to this core belief about your child.

> My belief is that the child comes to us perfect and complete.

In truth, we really do not know the true essence of wisdom (or genius) and where it forms. One's soul has so much to do with it and yet in society in general the more popular view is that we tend treat children like they are empty containers to be filled in rather than step aside and allowing their inherent wisdom to pour forth. Of course, there are cultures and religions that have a different view but they do not make up the mainstream majority. Over 500 years ago, Galileo said:

> *"You cannot teach a man anything; you can only help him find it within himself."*

It is already there. It is a part of the package. The child is already full and complete. Yet we have continued to ignore this, thinking that we can somehow improve what is already a perfect system.

Determining what is good for us has, for many millions of years, been managed by the infinitely more refined and knowledgeable areas of the mind called instinct. We come wired with it. It is a part of our operating system that we inherit as human beings on this planet. After all, we are mammals like so many other creatures of this earth.

But we are also human beings. And that definition is debated in all areas; science, faith, religion, beliefs, culture, race, location, socio-economic status, education, background, history, body, mind, spirit and so much more.

And each one of us is unique. We build on and change and expand as we go. We adapt upon our journey and each person has different elements to their personal journey. We are continually unconsciously collecting data, making observations, and calculations, and syntheses, and executions, more or less simultaneously and correctly and all of these millions of things going on all form our learning capabilities.

Yes. This is what we do, who we are, and yet, still, we act as though human nature were something to be afraid of; to constrain, to improve, to modify, to restrict, to fight, to subdue, to overcome, to conquer, to train, to bring up and to control. To control.

Somehow we have gotten so far away from believing that we are perfect. That we are incredible walking and talking miracles and that we do evolve in a way that works, automatically and without any interference.

We have instead had to spend our lifetimes believing that our nature has to be modified, opposed and controlled from the very beginning.

Stop.

Why do you think your child needs school in order to learn?

Our nature, like that of every other animal,
works just fine the way it is.

So what if we just accept that everything is as it should be. That we are perfect. That your child is perfect. Period.

Make your new belief be '*my child is perfect*'. How easy is that? Now imagine living that way. It's evident to me, that 99% of your stress would probably just disappear if you adopted this belief. My child is perfect, and you know what... so am I.

> *"Accept the children the way we accept trees - with gratitude, because they are a blessing - but do not have expectations or desires. You don't expect trees to change, you love them as they are."*
>
> *- Isabel Allende*

How empowering is that? How beautiful and healing. How EASY. What class or school or teacher can ever do something better than that? Or improve on that core belief. No one I know...

2

THE PERFECT CHILD

What if where you are now, where your child is now, is exactly where you are supposed to be? What if the only thing you are supposed to be doing is to be aware of the present moment? Miracles do happen in that space and they happen all of the time.

> **Note:** Make sure to check out the film 'Everyday Grace' with Marianne Williamson.

But we do not trust human nature. We distrust human nature in our children, and we distrust human nature in ourselves. And we do not think we are perfect. Old belief systems made us feel guilty, ashamed to even have such thoughts. We believe ourselves to be selfish, egotistical and bad for thinking we are perfect.

"Nobody's perfect".

I disagree.

What if what they told us was wrong? What if the '*nobody's perfect*' is actually a lie, a myth? What if what they meant to say is 'everyone is perfect' and they even sent a memo, but you were so busy you missed it! And because you missed it, you are still giving your children the old information? And because you did not get the memo, you are stuck in the old operating system.

And now you are passing this being stuck-ness onto your child. (*I know that is not a word, but it sounds good!*)

Let me remind you of a simple fact...

A child exists in a growing physical form, manifesting. A child is a process, a process of growth - we all are actually - but it is more obvious in the size and shape of a child. Evolution does happen, but it moves slowly and on a rhythm of its own, and it cannot be hurried.

Grab yourself a copy of *The Disappearance of Childhood* by Neil Postman and look at the obvious signs. Life is moving fast, but the rhythm and pulse of life remains constant, an ebb and flow with its own mysterious evolving.

It has not properly prepared today's children - forced to grow up so fast - and to conform to so many rules and regulations, and time schedules and tests. Their human nature and instinct has its own drives and needs, its own schedule and yet we impose a man-made regimen upon our child.

Am I saying we are going against nature when we do this? Yes. I am. Childhood has an unfolding of its own, much like a flower. Yes, we can now even force growth and when a plant blossoms, but at what cost?

This man-made regimen is a very new idea in the whole history of all humankind. Yet we believe it is superior to what human nature is and so we make our children adhere to our strict regimens and schedules.

We have to work, so we send them to school. Where else would they go? And, we have been told that is where they learn.

> *"My grandmother wanted me to have an education, so she kept me out of school."*
>
> *- Margaret Mead*

Ooops, it looks like we may have missed another memo. The one that says children learn all of the time, everywhere. They are sponges taking it all in.

Let me ask you this, if they go to school to learn, then what are they doing at home? Do they just lie in some strange limbo where learning is placed on hold? I mean, think about it. If they learn at school then at home is recreation? What are they doing at home? Existing? Wasting time? Vegging out? Not learning?

If you can 'see' learning, and you are convinced that it only happens at school then do you 'not see' learning at home? I know it sounds illogical and ridiculous, and yet that is how most people run their lives. They don't think about how ridiculous it is, they just go through the motions as if on auto-pilot.

What if there was a new memo that alerted you to think about the natural cycle of development and then the eight hour lock down of your child in an often fenced in, rigidly controlled, factory like environment. You know the look, kind of like a prison.

What if I took it another step further (*and this will really piss some people off*) and said that based on what we know about the natural development of human beings, school actually provides an abusive and demeaning experience that is against the natural instincts and nature of a growing child.

A prison like place where they have all been sentenced to do hard time for the bulk of their childhood (and most formative years) simply because they are children. Segregated like a completely different class of human being, discriminated because of their age and lack of having their own rights.

Hmm, something to think about. So what is it about schooling that I disagree with so passionately? Well, it is a bit complex. To even open this can of worms we have to look at the same in principle as when I was teaching my home birth classes.

You would first have to acknowledge what that you have been told all along is a lie so that your mind will even open to the possibility that there is an alternative.

But if your child's life is at stake, isn't it worth your discomfort?

Therefore, my recommendation before I go into deep conversation with anyone on the subject is to first read the following three books. And really, this is a must because if you are having the schooling vs. unschooling argument without processing true facts, research and data, then you are just spewing out your opinion, which is interesting, but not what is needed when making such a big decision.

> *Dumbing Us Down: The Hidden Curriculum of Compulsory Schooling* by John Taylor Gatto
> *Weapons of Mass Instruction: A Schoolteacher's Journey Through the Dark World of Compulsory Schooling* by John Taylor Gatto
> *The Underground History of American Education* by James Graham & John Taylor Gatto

When you do your homework, you will understand that John Taylor Gatto came to the conclusion that "compulsory schooling does little but teach young people to follow orders like cogs in an industrial machine." Yup. Cogs in an industrial machine. Ever think of your child as a cog before?

> **Note:** I refer to he or him or even little Jimmy in this book, but it is meant as he or she, him or her and little <insert name of your own child here> I just use that for ease of my own writing and mean no discrimination or separation.

Now before you get all up in arms, please realize that Mr. Gatto has been a teacher for 30+ years and is a recipient of the New York State Teacher of the Year award.

Again, I am not against all schooling, I am for learning and there is a huge difference. Schooling, as it exists in today's public school system is set up and *designed against learning.*

Read that again, it is not a typo. Schooling, as it exists in today's public school system is set up and designed against learning. It exists for the corporate interests and not in the best interests of your child.

> *"In the first place God made idiots. This was for practice. Then he made school boards."*
> - *Mark Twain*

But first you must understand how children really learn, and a great book I recommend on that subject is *How Children Learn* by John Holt.

John Holt was the first to make clear that, for small children, "learning is as natural as breathing" and he presents this idea again and again in all of his books. I recommend reading all of John's works.

If you are still with me and have read this far, you may be getting very uncomfortable.

Take them out of schools? Cogs in an industrial machine?

Those are some pretty strong opinions and ideas. But coming from a Teacher of the Year? With established research, statistics and evidence? Perhaps just to have an open mind, you should delve a bit deeper, go a little further down the rabbit hole.

What this illustrates is that I am not the only one with this opinion or position, and as each year passes, more and more people are pulling their children out of schools and voicing their own negative experiences with schools.

Parents. Teachers. Educators. And the ones who are speaking out all agree that schools today are broken. That is a fact.

Why? I am not sure why, and I do not even need to know. If something is broken, you move on. If your bicycle had a broken wheel a wheel which crashed and changed its shape into a square that did not roll easily, would you carry it or try to ride it home?

I think they why is not that important. What is important is that the child has natural needs and those needs are not being met at school.

Just the structure of school is offensive. I would not want to be forced to sit there.

Imagine... There is a teacher who knows it all and is the omnipotent LAW of the room. What she says goes. Period. If you ask a question, you are making trouble by questioning the authority. The children have to physically raise their hands to be allowed to speak or ask permission to go to the bathroom.

Don't you agree that this is demeaning for a human being?

We cringe at the sight of 'poor dogs' at shelters, and yet our poor children are also in a cage all day. They cannot do what they want, they must sit there, usually in an assigned seat and they have to do this for most of the useful hours of their day. They are filled with information that does not interest them and which they will probably never use in their own lives. They are force-fed whatever the curriculum or the teacher places in front of them for their consumption.

> *"Spoon feeding in the long run teaches us nothing but the shape of the spoon."*
>
> *- Edward M. Forster*

Today, corporations have interests in schools. Textbooks and learning materials have brands showing up in them and are written using NLP language to breed a specific kind of consumer. Study materials are written in a way to formulate social opinion and children are raised to be a very specific kind of citizen. This has nothing to do with being a good neighbor or a contributing member of your community. It has more to do with massive marketing and commercial interests.

"In 1896 the famous John Dewey, then at the University of Chicago, said that independent, self-reliant people were a counter-productive anachronism in the collective society of the future. In modern society, people would be defined by their associations and not by their own individual accomplishments. In such a world, people who read too well or too early are dangerous because they become privately empowered, they know too much, and know how to find out what they don't know by themselves, without consulting experts." (Kurt Johmann wrote that, quoting John Taylor Gatto.)

Kurt Johmann is a software developer who lives in Florida. He insists that American public schools teach a hidden curriculum of seven lessons:

1. Confusion. This includes a lack of subject-related context for what is actually being taught; too many unrelated facts and unrelated subjects; and a lack of meaning and critical thinking about what is taught.

2. Class Position. Students are kept in the same class by age, and, within this age classification, further classified and separated depending on how the students have done school wise *(for example, classification into so-called gifted classes)*. About this lesson John Taylor Gatto says: "That's the real lesson of any rigged competition like school. You come to know your place."

3. Indifference. Consider the effects of the ringing bell that announces the end of the current class and the need of your child to immediately whatever he is doing and proceed to the next class where a different teacher and subject await him. About the ringing bells John Taylor Gatto says: "Indeed, the lesson of bells is that no work is worth finishing, so why care too deeply about anything?"

4. Emotional Dependency. In school your child must submit to the designated authority, the teacher, and completely disregard their own personal desires during class (school) time. John Taylor Gatto says: "By stars and red checks, smiles and frowns, prizes, honors, and disgraces, I teach kids to surrender their will to the predestined chain of command." By the time this learned tendency reaches adulthood, it prevents many people from realizing there may be more qualified candidates other than the two corporate-approved rivals for any given office.

5. Intellectual Dependency. This lesson is similar to the lesson of emotional dependency, since both lessons teach students submission to the designated authority. In the case of the lesson of intellectual dependency, the students specifically learn submission to establishment authorities, including the teacher, on intellectual matters. This definitely discourages thinking "outside the box" when alternatives are presented to any given problem.

John Taylor Gatto says: "Successful children do the thinking I assign them with a minimum of resistance and a decent show of enthusiasm. Of the millions of things of value to study, I decide what few we have time for, or actually it is decided by my faceless employers. Bad kids fight this, of course, even though they lack the concepts to know what they are fighting, struggling to make decisions for themselves about what they will learn and when they will learn it. How can we allow that and survive as schoolteachers? Fortunately (*Gatto is being ironic*) there are tested procedures to break the will of those who resist".

> **6. Provisional Self-Esteem.** The lesson of report cards, grades, and tests is that children should not trust themselves or their parents but should instead rely on the evaluation of certified officials. They learn that people need to be told what they are worth. As a result, when people get older, they may not be able to determine the worth of a given activity without someone whose authority they covet approving their decision. Put more simply, they may not be able to think for themselves.

> **7. One Cannot Hide.** Constant surveillance teaches children they are watched by teachers and other school employees. They are always being watched. John Taylor Gatto says the underlying reason for this surveillance is that "children must be closely watched if you want to keep a society under tight central control. Children will follow a private drummer if you can't get them into a uniformed marching band."

When you read that, do you find yourself wondering how many passions have been lost to students who were told their natural aptitudes were leading them in the "wrong" direction, and whose talents were blunted by the corporate-approved drive toward regimented conformity?

Aside from teaching this hidden curriculum, the fact is that the schools also separate children from their families. By doing this, they weaken the traditionally held sacred bonds of the family.

This blatant and obvious attack against the family is a part of the larger campaign in America to atomize people into individuals, so that having only themselves, they are weak and helpless and unable to resist the establishment.

You know those individuals, right? The a-holes who walk around with a sense of entitlement that screams out "me", "me", "me", and yet who are unhappy, have no sense of self-worth and just keep whining on how much better it would be if they had more or whatever the guy across on the other side with the greener grass has...

Sound horrible? It is.

Yet we accept school, because that is where children go to learn and education is important. That is what we were told (*or sold*). Just like we were taught, we teach our own to "be good and go to school". No one ever offered an alternative.

> *"There is nothing on earth intended for innocent people so horrible as a school."*
>
> *- George Bernard Shaw*

Did we know alternatives existed? Maybe our own education (*training*) got in the way and that is why we never even had a question about it. After all, teacher taught us that questions are bad. Troublemakers ask questions...

You may think the above is radical but perhaps the most thought provoking work I have found to date is a collection of essays by Ivan Illich published in 1970.

Decades ahead of his time, he predicts exactly what is occurring with technology and schooling today.

His book scared me, shocked me and supported me during many long nights of wondering if I had chosen the right path.

In reading *Deschooling Society* by Ivan Illich, I found incredible truth in his predictions and the course of my life, forever changed.

A reviewer summed it up best when writing "This is a heartfelt series of essays that illuminate the nature of learning and the perverse consequences of professionally imposed schooling requirements. Far from the assumed engine of equality, modern schooling promotes inequality and social stratification.

It's powerful and graded liturgy convinces the majority of people that their inferior status derives from a failure to consume sufficient quantities of expensive educational services. Illich links schooling and modern ideas of education to the belief in endless progress and the ultimate abolition of 'Necessity'. What starts out as a program in humanism ends up as a formula for the destruction of what it is to be human."

Perverse consequences are what we are seeing with school shootings, and ten year olds committing suicide.

Our children are supposed to be experiencing what it means to be human and alive, not to be in a dysfunctional toxic hell of perversion of the human experience.

"Let's make the schools better then!"

The conversation I propose is not about how schools can be improved. I believe we are beyond that.

It is about children being able to fully experience their own lives, purpose, and journey.

Childhood demands freedom and needs it to allow a well-developed and happy adult to blossom. Schools are prisons that strip this away from children in order to make them a specific kind of citizen and proper follower.

> *"Anyone who has passed through the regular gradations of a classical education, and is not made a fool by it, may consider himself as having had a very narrow escape."*
>
> *- William Hazlitt*

I am not simply advocating making adjustments to teaching methods. In fact, I do not even want to give directions on how to move away from school and to a homeschool environment. Maybe 15 years ago, that was my position. But more study, more research and more experience would now have me share that it is the whole idea of a place called school or the act of teaching that needs to be rethought.

The bottom line and what I found in my research...

School is not a good place for a growing child. In fact, it is the worst place for any child to be.

And how do we even know that what they are teaching will be relevant in such a rapidly changing world?

Since we can't know what knowledge will be most needed in the future, it is senseless to try to teach it in advance. Instead, we should try to turn out people who love learning so much and learn so well that they will be able to learn whatever must be learned.

> *"It is in fact nothing short of a miracle that the modern methods of instruction have not yet entirely strangled the holy curious of inquiry. It is a very grave mistake to think that the enjoyment of seeing and searching can be promoted by means of coercion and a sense of duty."*
>
> *- Albert Einstein*

Ivan Illich's research is interesting as well. It tells us that 'schooling converts verbs into nouns in our lives'.

The modern educational system is created by and in turn promotes a constant reification, a constant restructuring of every intangible human capacity into a tangible need - into a consumer demand for service to be supplied by some institutional provider.

Our lives have been hijacked by a consumer mentality and this indoctrination begins in school.

> *"Education is one of the chief obstacles to intelligence
> and freedom of thought."*
>
> *- Bertrand Russell*

Illich writes, 'Schooling is failing to do what it promised - to educate in any broad sense, to bring up the poor and better their condition, to do any of this without ever-growing bureaucracies and ballooning budgets. In fact, formal schooling has become a largely self-perpetuating juggernaut that seems more content with perpetuating a belief in its necessity than actually facilitating learning.' (*Learning, of course, being defined as something a bit broader than just absorbing the teachings of credentialed teachers*).

Learning is about more than the A, B, and C's.

It is about life and being human.

So I ask you, is your child supported in being human and alive in school? Do the teachers care about his humanness and aliveness?

Do you, the parent, truly feel in your deepest core that you are experiencing being truly human and alive? Or are you still waiting for someone or something to make you complete, make you whole?

Yes, that is what those who believe a child needs to be filled up believe – and with that belief, they are doing their best to fill up the child, because after all, the child comes empty and needs to be filled up, right?

But what of the instinct of the child? And let's take it even deeper than that – what of the inner life of the child, *meaning the soul*, the spirit or the essence of the Divine within the child?

Does your belief system have a place for soul, spirit, or life force – or Source? And if so, do we need to fill that too?

What does that experience look or feel like in the institution of school?

Or maybe that has no place in school.

School should then be what? Mechanical? Maybe then, you also believe that your child is a machine, an empty container, or as Gatto put it, 'a cog in the machine'?

This can go round and round and I have been there with many parents who I've consulted. They want to hear the argument against school, because they are not happy with their child in school, but then auto-pilot sets in and I am back again in the childbirth classes with the home birthing episode.

To accept the new truth, one has to first admit that the old truth was a falsehood. Now, don't get me wrong - I believe we are all growing and learning along the way. Maybe the falsehood was a truth at one point. But that does not mean it must remain a truth forever.

My personal belief is that the inner life of a child in school is one of a wounded and confused being who cannot comprehend why his cries for the fulfillment of his innate expectations go unanswered. And then he is made wrong by the teacher for having natural instincts and expectations. Worse still, he is punished to ask or question at all. Finally, who is he to even matter? Why should anything or anyone matter?

And we ask why children are committing murder and suicide?

From this belief, is it any wonder then, that the children develop a sense of wrongness and shame about themselves? About their desires and interests and needs? What happens when this takes place? Where does the child store these feelings and these impressions? Do they just dissipate into the ethers or does the child carry them in an imaginary bag that he drags around.

Maybe he stores them all in his mind that then places pressure on other parts of the mind, or maybe it activates feelings in the child which influence his behavior. Maybe this is why a child bullies, commits suicide or shoots his fellow school mates. Not *maybe* but surely.

Or maybe that is just too extreme – maybe the child just sits obediently and learns to smile and pretend those feelings and impressions do not exist, until much later in life where it manifests as addiction, rage or a quiet apathy and lack of self-worth.

Kytka Hilmar-Jezek

"Education is the period during which you are being instructed by somebody you do not know, about something you do not want to know."

- Gilbert K. Chesterton

In my experience, children who are seen and heard and encouraged to be curious, grow up to have greater self-esteem and become more independent than those who are expected to sit, be still, obedient and be quiet.

This has to go back to some toxic dysfunction rooted in the parenting Dr. Spock style and that whole generation.

- Feed them on a schedule
- Let them cry it out
- Don't let them manipulate you - or you may spoil them or make them too dependent.

That is absolute garbage. No child is born rotten, or manipulative, or spoiled. You just don't have bad children. It's not true. It's a myth. There is no such thing. But we can make them "bad" with twisted and corrupted archaic beliefs that there is some proper way to raise them up.

Why do we try to fix things that are not broken? Why do we try to improve on magnificent nature?

Consider this...

They grow on their own and if allowed to unfold naturally, they actually thrive and they blossom quite beautifully.

Let them be.

3

EXTINCTION

If you know the work of Jean Liedloff who wrote the beautiful book entitled *The Continuum Concept: In Search Of Happiness Lost* then you know that all babies have a very real need to be next to a warm, breathing, live human body.

If you have not read the book, I recommend you read it. Even if your children are older, reading it will give you some insight as to why your child may be exhibiting some attention getting behaviors now.

> *The little ones who are crying, this very moment, unanimously – all over the world to voice their anger at the denial of what is their basic human need at this stage. And they will not stop until they physically exhaust themselves and even then it will not go away – because they are driven by something they cannot turn off, and something that we cannot train out of them by keeping a rigid schedule – they are driven by an instinct to survive, and to survive, they need physical human contact.*
>
> *- The Continuum Concept by Jean Liedloff*

The baby knows what he needs, and the minute you put him down, he cries. He does not know or understand that you had plans at that moment or that you have to go to work.

His evolution says that he is supposed to alert and remind you not to let him down.

He is perfectly doing what nature intended him to do.

So he continues to signal you perfectly, clearly, "don't put me down!"

And our instinct says when baby cries, pick him up. Do not put him down.Do not leave the baby.

But media, culture, society – they say go to work, go to dinner, go to the gym, go get your nails done. Our faith in our own instincts is undermined right from birth.

Dr. Spock tells us "Don't let that spoiled brat manipulate you – who is the grown up here?" He shames you and speaks down at you with imagined pointed finger shaking into your face. And he becomes the "expert" and he is known the world over.

There is no "expert" in the natural process.You don't see the natural process on television and in magazines.

> Hint: there is no money to be made in the natural process and television and magazines run on advertising dollars from people trying to sell you something. Just because it is on television or in magazines does not make it useful or true.

There is no support. Instead, you see ads for cribs, playpens, stroller, baby monitors and complete nursery rooms.

You see medicines for postpartum depression. You see escapism and frustration. Special mommy groups form, where moms meet to get away from the little manipulator at home who is driving them crazy.

"Gee - no one told me they cry all night long! I can't handle it!" And people connect like this and they reaffirm beliefs that are outdated, archaic and simply wrong.

They are wrong not because of a judgment, they are wrong because they do not function, and they do not function because they are against human nature.

But no one told them there was / is another way...

Had we lived a mere 200 years ago, the elders would have known that to quiet a baby, simply hold it. They knew that a baby is actually simple because it has only two needs; to be in arms and to have access to the breast.

The child was a blessing then and was in the arms of all the people in the village. When not in arms, the child was gently sleeping in some sort of a sling draped over mothers shoulder as she went about her daily work...

Life was not too fast, not too fast for childhood. The people then knew then that children have a job and it was understood by all that their job was important. It was the job of an adventurer and an explorer. And it was the most important job. This was the "work" of the child, and all understood to not disturb the important work of the child.

When children asked questions, the adults answered with patience. They were proud to do their part in contributing to the repertoire of knowledge for the child. And the child grew, understanding that different people saw the same things in different ways. Some made sense to the child and felt good, others seemed strange and the child could decide that information was not for him or would not work in his own life. In this way, the child became human.

The child was allowed to freely go around and sample, taste, touch, experience. There were no electrical sockets that needed to be plugged in with plastic plugs, no streets that needed to be avoided with fast cars or potential kidnappers or predators.

The world was smaller, closer, more intimate and safer. It was a world much friendlier to children and for the growing of human beings.

Faces were as familiar as was the territory and the worst thing a child put into its mouth was a bug (*which probably wasn't too tasty so usually it was spit right out again*), and the child continued tasting, touching and feeling until it found a soft lap to sit on or to watch the rhythmic work of someone going about their daily tasks.

This is the life of childhood.

And sadly, today it is almost extinct.

Can your child run out the door and into the yard to find

grandpa working with wood and grandma sitting and knitting on the porch? Will he see mother kneeling in the garden and father tending to the animals?

I doubt it.

So where will this child go to have this development take place? Will the child grow up undeveloped?

If the child does not get this, will he go around empty or will the space meant for all of this be filled with something else? Something artificial, something of lesser value, something that will change the kind of adult this child grows into?

4

SPONGES

Yes, the world has changed. Now a child is no longer welcomed to be an adventurer or an explorer. The child can no longer safely wander.

"Don't touch, it's dirty,"

"Be careful, you'll hurt yourself,"

"Don't do that, you'll break it!"

Tragically, this is the new language for children. Language and expectation which not only goes against a child's human nature and natural instinct to wander and explore, but also which constantly undermines the child's feeling of competence and trust in his own instincts.

"I'm stupid." "This sucks."

Childhood now, has become a dangerous place that needs to be restricted, controlled and shut off, shut away. Shame.

But nature follows its natural course. The child's world does expand and soon the child gets to go to school. The child is happy, filled with the anticipation of following the natural instinct. But all too soon, the child will hear words that don't make sense.

He hears words that go against the nature inside of him.

"Sit still."

"Fold your hands."

"Don't talk to your neighbor"

"Don't ask questions."

"Wrong answer."

"Don't interrupt me."

"Be quiet."

The child comes home and we tell them how they have to be good in school, and how to be good in church and at the store and at grandma's house, and on and on....

We never for a moment trust that they ARE good. Instead we have this idea that we have to tell them to BE good. And the child's mind is naturally inquisitive, so he questions it.

"Why do they have to tell me to be good? Am I so bad?"

And no adult really stops to think about his or her words, we just assume on auto-pilot that we know it all, not even re-alizing that when we do this, what we are really saying is that they should just *pretend* to be good. Because if we thought some-one WAS good then we wouldn't need to tell them to BE good, would we?

"You are in kindergarten children, now be good.".

"You are going to your play date at Jimmy's house, so be good." "We are going shopping now, so be good".

Sometimes it is more of a threat than a command.

"You better be good at grandma's house".

The child figures out rather quickly that what that really means is to *pretend to be good* because they know what children really are, and that is bad.

Imagine that. Imagine how your child feels being told to "be good" over and over and over and over and over again. And it's not just the parents. It is as though all of the adults jump on board with the "be good" message. This lousy message is repeat-ed time and time again, like brainwashing!

The tragic thing is that it goes straight to the heart of a child like a poisonous arrow. It goes to his deepest feelings of self-worth; where his self-confidence is being formed. That is a tricky place - a place that can really screw us up as adults if not dealt with gently and carefully. But there is no time for that.

Rrrring... There is the bell, time to think about the next sub-ject. But wait – that was beginning to interest me. I think I may have been onto something...

Pattern interrupt. Life interrupt.

Children just have to spend all of their time "being good". And as they grow it forms. This strange feeling that says "I've got to learn to hide what I really am. I'm bad but I'd better try to look good to get by."

> *"I loathed every day and regret every moment I spent in a school."*
>
> - *Woody Allen*

Like Pavlov's dogs, children are conditioned to keep doing of what is expected to get by for the rewards of acceptance, praise, gold stars and love. Note that I didn't say unconditional love, because after all, the condition is that love only comes when we "be good".

This is not the life of a human being as designed by evolution, by nature or by instinct. This is a man-made cage and in it the human lives the life of a slave or a trained dog or experimental monkey.

It is ugly. So ugly that most people don't want to look at it. To look at it may activate that "everything I thought was true was a lie" feeling and we all know what happens when we do that.

Perhaps an important core question a parent should always ask is "Do I want my child *to learn* or to be *trained* to appear that he is learning." Now remember this though, whatever children are doing —they are *learning all the time*, like little sponges.

Rrrrring..... Did you just hear the bell? We have to get back to school. So in this place called school, the children are told, "Stop doing what you want to do because it is worthless." They continue: "What IS important is this. Now pay attention, be good."

The children are force fed all that "IS important". The school said so. Who cares that the child would rather imagine interesting and creative ways to make discoveries in science, physics or technology? They are at a specific grade level and for ALL children at this grade level, the school decided what is important.

The saddest thing is that today the teacher has very little to do with it. At least 20 or 30 years ago we had a good teacher here and there. Today they are all giving tests and dishing out the common core. A government set and mandated set of standards. One size fits all.

I think Mr. Anthony Esolen describes it best in his book *Life Under Compulsion: Ten Ways To Destroy the Humanity in Your Child* when he writes the following:

"The chief lesson that the bell teaches is that all things must serve a utilitarian purpose. I recall reading in The Princeton Alumni Weekly, an insufferable publication of my alma mater, about how a woman managed time with her small boy. He was allowed to approach the Presence between three and three-thirty, but then he had to leave, because Mummy had important work to do, evidently far more important than was the small boy. But also more important than Mummy herself. The bell says, 'Nothing is of ultimate concern, because all things end when I determine.'

There are only two reasons why one would study a thing that is not of ultimate concern, or that does not bring that delight that carries us out of ourselves, as experiences of love and beauty do. One is that it is useful, a means to a farther end. The other is that we have no choice. We are compelled to do it. And since the experience of love or of beauty is by its nature impossible to compel, any justification for the compulsion must rest on utilitarian grounds. But that reduces education to a tool, and a tool which is often of dubious quality.

That is right and just, since the children themselves are tools of dubious quality. They are called *our greatest resource*, like a deposit of tin. They are treated as advance troops in the remaking of the human material known as their parents. They are educated, not as persons made in the image and likeness of the living God, but as pawns in a vast sociopolitical game; they too are not valued in themselves and for themselves, but for what they will accomplish. They will be rewarded according to how well they adapt themselves to the Teaching Machine, whose judgments are at once lax (for the Machine does not actually teach a great lot) and severe (for the judgments enter the Book of Life, with implications for college and employment thereafter, worldliness without end)."

A truly incredible book. Who is to say that there is one particular body of knowledge that every person, regardless of the life they lead, needs to possess.

From the Common Core State Standards Initiative: "The Common Core is a set of high-quality academic standards in mathematics and English language arts/literacy (ELA). These learning goals outline what a student should know and be able to do at the end of each grade. The standards were created to ensure that all students graduate from high school with the skills and knowledge necessary to succeed in college, career, and life, regardless of where they live."

One size fits all. Pay attention. Are you paying attention?

Poor children, over and over again being told to pay attention, especially when something interesting caught their eye outside the window – the clouds moving in a faster way than usual and getting darker and heavier. A storm must be coming....

"Are you paying attention?"

As if the child does not naturally want to pay attention and learn. (*That is all they do as children.*)

Sometimes I wonder if this constant implication that the child is not paying attention may directly coincide with the attention deficit labels, but that is a whole other conversation isn't it.

> "*One had to cram all this stuff into one's mind, whether one liked it or not. This coercion had such a deterring effect that, after I had passed the final examination, I found the consideration of any scientific problems distasteful to me for an entire year.*"
>
> *- Albert Einstein*

Back to NOW PAY ATTENTION..... 'A' is for apple." Correct? "Yes... correct". Do we all agree?

This is how it works in school. Everything else is undermined and pronounced worthless because "A" is for apple. Period.

Heck, you can type "a is for" into Google and a whole bunch of apples shows up. Enough to fill a whole bushel of apples!

But what if for me, "A" isn't for apple? What if, for me, "A" is for ambulance or "A" is for adventure or "A" is for airplane?

It is likely that 'A' can be for as many different things as there are different people - but in school there is usually only one right answer and that is that "A" is for apple. The child who wants to believe that "A" is for angel is making trouble.

"Troublemaker."

"You are being bad."

"Smartass!"

"In school, 'A' is for apple."

"Be good."

It's not good to think outside the box. "A" is for apple and apple only. That's just the way it is. But what if "A" IS for angel? The child is constantly made to be wrong, and when he wants to say that 'A' is for angel - he is bad, and rude, and a disturbance.

I know that what that child really wants is to shout out, and loud for the world to hear. He wants to scream out "'A' is for ACCEPT me, 'A' is for APPRECIATE me, 'A' is for ALLOW ME to BE me."

But the teachers tell you no. "A" is for apple and nothing else counts. Put angel on your test and you fail. Nothing else gets the point, the gold star or the passing grade. You need to get the correct answer. "A" is for apple and nothing else in the entire dictionary matters. Nothing else in the world matters.

Personally, I get mental imagery of the teacher who liked wrapping the children's knuckles with his ruler in the film Pink Floyd's '*The Wall*' and I think "A" is for asshole... but that does not matter.

(*Oh, get over it! I use shocking pattern interrupts and language patterns on purpose to try to get people to think. If you want to judge the information and my because I wrote 'asshole' then you were just looking for an excuse to close this book now because you are in the uncomfortable zone of having to admit that what you knew to be true is maybe not true and this is just too much for some.)*

Perhaps the question we need to ask ourselves is does the educational establishment produce individuals who can actually think, or is the end product someone who can reproduce the "correct answer"?

Monkey see, monkey do.

Good doggie.

Give him a treat.

I think Paul Goodman said it best when he said "Given their present motives, the schools are not competent to teach authentic literacy, reading as a means of liberation and cultivation. And I doubt that most of us who seriously read and write the English language ever learned it by the route of `Run, Spot, Run'."

> *"Underneath the visible problems with reading and writing lies the deeper problem of 'illearnacy': an acquired disabling of learning courage and learning initiative."*
>
> *- Guy Claxton, 'Wise Up'*

Yet this redundant "A" is for apple brainwashing is the day in the life of a child in school. Day after day, week after week, month after month, year after year. This is what your child is committed to, every day.

Would you find it bearable?

For "support" you have an entire gang of parents, teachers, society - all of these authority figures - telling you and reaffirming over and over and over again that you and that your true inherent nature - and birthright, which is to explore and to learn automatically and on your own - is worthless. It's not the "right way". It's not important. It does not matter.

They insist if "they" don't teach you, it's not learning.

And they remind you that children *need* to learn and that is why they *have* to go to school. But that is a blatant LIE. Children learn ALL OF THE TIME.

In fact, we all do our entire lives. A human is constantly learning and evolving. That function comes with the human being automatically. It's not even an add-on package, it's included with every model.

> *"I am beginning to suspect all elaborate and special systems of education. They seem to me to be built up on the supposition that every child is a kind of idiot who must be taught to think."*
>
> *- Anne Sullivan*

But those who have been too busy to think for themselves because they've been at work and at school, they have not been told there is light on the other side.

They are still reading Dr. Spock. They are running their program on a code that is outdated and has been hacked by so many viruses and their family has broken down.

They are unhappy, their children are unhappy and they are so far removed from what they had envisioned "family" would look like, they live in despair, trying to fill themselves up with an endless calendar filled with distractions so they do not have to face the feelings of failure.

Did they fail? No – they didn't. They have only been misinformed. They are running an old program.

> **Note:** There is a much better replacement today for evil Dr. Spock. Dr. Sears has gained popularity the last decade or so and his books provide more humanistic value to new parents. Look him up and study what he has to offer...

Sometimes the answers we seek are not complex at all. Sometimes they can come in a quote, a sign, a simple story...

An excellent children's book on being afraid to think as an individual and having the courage to face what's on the other side is called *Grasper: A Young Crabs Discovery* by Paul Owen Lewis. It is a children's book. It can be read in all of about five minutes. Yet the lesson is profound. Grasper contains a wonderful story to share with a child.

From the book description: "A crab comes out of his shell, travels beyond his small, comfortable world, and brings back an inspirational message of possibility and courage to his fellow crabs who remained in the old tide pool."

Interesting concept.

I recommend the read.

5

HUMAN SURVIVAL

Let's have a quick history lesson, because after all – the learning happens all of the time and it comes with the package as an add-on, remember? We may as well use it every now and again!

So when did the family break down? Was it natural?

If you love history and love research as much as I do, your will come across some pretty interesting bits of information if you begin to research.

Professor Ruth Wisse, from Harvard wrote:

"Women's Liberation, if not the most extreme, then certainly the most influential neo-Marxist movement in America, has done to the American home what communism did to the Russian economy, and most of the ruin is irreversible. By defining between men and women in terms of power and competition instead of reciprocity and co-operation, the movement tore apart the most basic and fragile contract in human society, the unit from which all other social institutions draw their strength."

She is speaking of the family.

Author Erin Pizzey wrote: "Family life was and always will be the foundation of any civilization. Destroy the family and you destroy the country."

Now obviously there is much, much more to that, but in a nutshell – when mothers left the home and placed the care of their children into impersonal holding cells such as daycare, the unraveling of family began and this only happened as a direct result of the industrial revolution.

Because for all of human history up to that point, the family unit was regarded as *a necessity to human survival.*

Family is being deconstructed and destroyed. And remember in the previous chapter, this is one of the hidden lessons of school. Rip the youth from the arms of their parents and send them to school. It used to be at the age of six, then five and now even sooner.

J. H. Van der Berg wrote: "Children go to school from the time they are four or five years old. By the time they leave school forever, they are no longer able to be educated, in the original meaning of the word. The sick are not nursed at home; even the chronically sick are removed from their families more and more frequently. The old people disappear into homes for the aged more often than in the past. This disappearance is felt to be necessary by both young and old: life changes so quickly and fundamentally that one cannot expect old people to adapt themselves continuously to the ways of their children.

Clothes are made at home less and less often. Food is not stored for the winter. Remedies are no longer prepared at home. Even recreation is sought elsewhere. Families who still give parties at home are becoming scarce. The custom of group singing, accompanied by the harmonica, violin, or guitar played by one of the family or a neighbor has died out - replaced by the relentless noise of a cackling or jingling contraption, recently brought to perfection by the addition of a screen, which has definitely put an end to all activity."

Of course, he wrote all of that before tablets, cellular phones, iPods and such; before kids were plugged into their on line world and video games. I cannot imagine what we would write if he were alive today.

Can you even imagine your life with all of the electricity turned off for a week, a month, a year?

Do you think you would be able to completely shut down all of the modern media that you have most likely grown so accustomed to? Because children learn by example, not by "do as I am told, not as I do".

Can you imagine your family living like they did over 100 years ago?

I challenge you to go there and spend a day. Go there in story if you cannot go there in real life. Go to the park or the beach, take the book, leave all distractions at home and enjoy...

A wonderful children's book to illustrate the need and love and commitment of family is called "*Sarah, Plain and Tall*" written by Patricia MacLachlan, the winner of the 1986 Newbery Medal and the 1986 Scott O'Dell Award for Historical Fiction.

The novel is set in the western United States during the late 19th century. About a man named Jacob Witting, a widowed farmer who is still saddened by the death of his wife during childbirth several years earlier finds that the task of taking care of his farm and two children, Anna and Caleb, is just too difficult to handle alone. He writes an ad in the newspaper for a mail-order bride.

Sarah, from Maine, answers his ad and travels out to become his wife. There are five books in this series about the Witting family and they are all lovely – and because so many people are too busy to even read these days, I'm so pleased Hallmark Films made the first 3 into movies which you can purchase on DVD. They are quality family entertainment with Glenn Close and Christopher Walken playing the lead roles.

Now you may be wondering what this has to do with schooling or education. I often refer to books or movies when I speak because we used to learn through the oral folk tradition. The story tellers weaved tales that spoke to our subconscious and embedded he codes of conduct, compassion, forgiveness, charity, contribution, love, acceptance – all of these virtues were woven into the fibers of our being by story.

These days we do not have the village weaver of tales, we have kindle tablets. But we do have books and film, and while a lot of what is made is just entertainment (*and junk entertainment at that*) there are also a lot of wonderful stories still being woven through film. Books of course, have always been sources of information.

The premise remains the same...

Through imagery, lessons can be learned that do not need to be lectured or forced and we learn them through story and in modern times, through film, just as through listening to story, feelings are invoked that connect to the senses and we feel things.

The Sarah series will make you feel a strong understanding of the need and the love and, above all, the value of family.

Reading the story and watching the film, you get a nostalgia for something that maybe you yourself have never known. The idea of an extended family, the community.

Another series to take you to the time of when people counted on each other for survival is the *"Little House on the Prairie"* series with Michael Landon. I told you, as children mine had no television. Now that they are older, we sometimes watch older television or film together. My daughters loved the Little House series and we ended up purchasing the DVDs of the pilot, the ten seasons and the after season film.

My children loved the story, but were frustrated that the way of life is not common anymore, especially in the United States.

When we went to Europe and Central America, they were impressed with the rural lifestyles we discovered there and they appreciated that we could have the experience, if even for a little while. But even so, we return home and they find themselves also being nostalgic.

Once again, J.H. van der Berg sums it up best with this from *The Changing Nature of Man.*

"Thinking of small groups, I am reminded, not without nostalgia, of the conversations on the steps in the backyard. In the front, houses might appear separate; but in the back, they used to have a common atmosphere which made differences of opinion not impossible, but which reached beyond them. And quarrels with one's neighbors were far more evidence of understanding than of difference.

Today neighbors seldom quarrel; people do not know one another well enough and are afraid to learn enough of each other to start an open war. In the old days they did; the words reverberated against the walls, everybody listened attentively and with satisfaction, everyone talked about it for a few days and then it was forgotten. Or else the quarrel turned into Stone and became part of the loosely-solid structure of the backyards, with their henhouses, their rabbit crates, their cats, and their tame crows.

During the summer on Saturday evenings and on Sundays, everybody was there, on the steps or leaning back on chairs, talking telling stories, and singing. When it grew dark the stories began to predominate. The children became quiet and listen until they were sent to bed, where they could still hear the voices for hours. The group existed, it was real.

When somebody fell ill he could count on help - on soup, on eggs or some fruit. The saying that a near neighbor is better than a distant cousin originated in those days. It is no longer true. For the neighbor has become a stranger who lives next door; greetings are exchanged, but we hardly talk with him and we certainly would not sing with him.

The distant cousin now has a car, and will be over in a few minutes. But he is gone in a few minutes, too, with his car; for he is busy. And for that matter, we had not kept in touch with him; actually, we had not seen him for years.

If we should fall ill now, it would be wiser to go to a hospital...."

What are we missing? What are we denying our children, and ourselves, by erasing such activities from our lives? I think it is a weave in the fabric of what makes us human.

Sitting together around the television set was warned against in Neil Postman's *"Amusing Ourselves To Death"*. At least at the time of his writing, we were all sitting around the television set together and would converse before or after the regularly scheduled programming.

Today, we all have our own hand held device. We are rarely in the same room. Mothers use monitors to peek at baby, they deny themselves and their baby the human contact.

A widening gap. Distance. Disconnect. Loneliness. Exile.

6

CHILDREN AS EXILES

But perhaps looking at "family" in the times of Sarah is an example which does not go back far enough. You have read some quotes by J.H. van der Berg and are likely wondering who he is. I think this chapter is the perfect place to introduce him properly.

Jan Hendrik van den Berg was a Dutch psychiatrist notable for his work in phenomenological psychotherapy and metabletics, or "psychology of historical change." He authored *The Changing Nature of Man.*

His overriding research interest was to systematically explore the changing nature of Western man, woman and children from the Middle Ages to the present time. His studies dealt with human existence as given in relationships within a specific historical time period and social cultural context. It addressed the world of men, women, and children in their relationships to each other, to things and to God. Each shift in what he called "a metabletic sense" meant that a phenomenon had changed in a significant way, and opened up a new way of life and a new meaning expressed simultaneously in diverse fields of human activity.

I cannot recommend reading the work enough and if you search Google for "The Changing Nature of Man" by J.H. van den Berg, you will find many free .pdf versions on line.

In *The Changing Nature of Man,* he writes

"We have said that the child lives in a separate world often enough. But perhaps these words are still too cautious and too theoretical to portray with enough clarity how separate this world really is. He who wants to see with his own eyes the separateness of the child's world, who wants to observe how the child is put down (lovingly) in a space of its own, cannot do better than visit a playground. He will have to adjust his eyes to the observation of certain peculiarities. Or rather, he must take off the glasses, which make all inevitabilities seem acts of love. What he will then observe is what I have described in this book: a fenced-in space, an island in the middle of the mature world, an island of comparative, safety in a fatal maturity, an island of (necessary) exile.

`When the child ventures on the street - he must go to school and come home again - he has to be armed against the dangers he will meet. The grownups have given him a crossing guard.

The children wait on the pavement until their group has grown big enough, then the guard puts up his hand, the traffic stops, and the group of exiles hurry to the other side of the street. No sooner is the last child off the street than the waiting traffic accelerates and hurries on.

A group of exiles? The thought that we are good for the children is more agreeable; so good are we that we lend them the attributes of maturity to defend themselves.

Look, there they go; everybody stops; the businessman, whose time is money, the large truck, whose delay can be expressed in hard cash - everybody stops for the children.

Are not we good to them? Doubtless we are, but it is the least we can do; we are obliged to be good to them, because of the great amount of irreparable evil we have done. Our goodness pays for a great injustice."

His work takes you all the way back to when there was no separation between adult and child. A time when these smaller, growing individuals were perceived in an entirely different way in the world.

As you read it, you will find it hard to believe because we have moved so far from those concepts, but at the same time, has this shift proved itself a step in the direction of progress?

I will leave you to consider that question yourself and ponder your answers.

He shares how children were an active part of daily life (and death) and because they were, they had a different level of maturity, of development, of responsibility and understanding.

For example, let's look at what he says about *The Invisibility of Modern Maturity*

"To the eyes of the child, maturity is invisible. In the past, if a child walked through the streets of his town, he could see and hear around him how trades were practiced, one of which trades he would choose himself later on. The rope-maker, the smith, the brazier, the cooper, the carpenter, they all worked in places accessible to any child: in their houses, in work yard, or somewhere in the open.

Today most trades are shut away in factories, where children are not allowed. How can a child know what happens there? His father, when he comes home from his work, brings with him at the most a story and a smell; no doubt these are important indications, but they are only indications: the reality itself remains invisible.

Besides, more and more jobs are coming into existence that are invisible to the child even if he does witness what is being done. What sort of an idea can the child have of his father's work if the father is a superintendent, a social worker, a tax collector, or a psychotherapist! And as for the last, what does my child think of the work I do? People called "patients," who do not appear to be ill at all, come at appointed hours and stay in my room sometime.

This does not tell him anything but that he has to be quiet while they are there and then they leave again. Can I expect my child to choose my profession? Obviously not; if he did, I should be justified in doubting the soundness of his choice, for he would be choosing an emptiness, a meaningless thing - a disappearance into a room, a silence, and a thoughtful reappearance. For this is what I show my children, nothing else.

That is why I feel reassured when I find that none of my children wants to be a psychotherapist. And I think that a tax collector, a social worker, and a superintendent should have the same feeling of relief when they find that their children are in agreement about this one thing - that they will never follow in their father's footsteps.

As long as I shut myself away in my office, I am negating what I have just said. I am invisible; there is no element of visibility, however small, which would allow my child to get an idea of my occupation.

The same thing applies to the factory worker's son; when his father leaves, the door dividing home from the outside world closes behind him, the son cannot accompany him (he would be killed in the traffic) and another door, the factory entrance, closes behind his father. Relentlessly. The son is not permitted inside (he might be caught in the machinery), and he cannot see anything of what his father does during the day - his father who falls in his chair in the evening and gets out his newspaper, saying, 'He was in a bloody temper,' meaning the boss, or, 'We've got a new radio in our department', meaning the music that gratified his ears when he was busy doing what his son will never see.

'What are you going to be' asks this father, when his son leaves school; to this question he will get the almost stereotyped reply, 'I don't know.'

'In my time,' says the father - certainly, in his time children knew at least a little of that choice; a few things were still visible.

But these fathers are getting scarce; they will die out.

Soon no father will be able to say, 'In my time we knew what we were going to be,' for nobody will remember ever having known, nobody will cherish the memory of an insecure, risky time in which a future was built on nothing, or rather on a few futile visibilities, on trifles - that is, on significant beacons.

Today one's occupation is prescribed by institutions which

have lately become necessary, which falsely suggest they are supplying an age-old deficiency.

This deficiency was apparently embodied in the happy-go-lucky choice, the choice made on a few silly visibilities, the choice without motives - and yet such a choice was never unmotivated. For true motives are not to be found in what is available - in what has been yesterday and can be inspected as an inventory today - but in what will be tomorrow. To make a choice is to be invited; and that is what making a choice meant then.

There will be choosing after making an inventory.

Soon, making a choice will mean choosing what appears as the most probable or the least impossible from an inventory. It is to be expected that making the inventory will be put off as long as possible, for something that might justify a choice does not exist. Nor did it exist in the past. The things which decided the choice then were not to be found in the person who was making the choice; they were outside of him, they were in the future.

Today they have to be found in the person who is making the choice; the future is empty. But the person who makes the choice is just as empty; no one starts life with a program.

So he will have to wait. 'You'll have to wait a little longer', says the expert to the mother. 'The child is still too immature. Let us put him through college first.'

And if he goes through college and he still does not know (this happens every day, even now) then the expert will have to say that the inventory is still deficient, the child is still not formed (how could he bell, he is still too playful (but how could he have acquired maturity?). 'Can't he go through another year of college?'

Ever putting it off: the children are empty."

> "Knowledge that is acquired under compulsion obtains no hold on the mind."
>
> - *Plato*

The essay was written in 1961.

Van den Berg shares throughout how the child in the Western world was seen for centuries as a little adult because he could both participate in and understand the adult world.

Up until the 17th century, daily life for adults and for children was relatively unified, accessible and comprehensible. However, over the course of the 18th century, life for both became gradually complex, learned and divided which made it increasingly invisible, inaccessible and incomprehensible. This was especially so for children who gradually slid out of the adult world and became children in the modern sense of the world with their own mode of being, thinking and feeling.

The last quarter of the 18th century saw not only the birth of childhood but also the birth of the modern family in contrast to the traditional family of the past.

The accelerated pace of change by the middle of the 20th century increased the complexity of society and its divisiveness which impacted on all of its members. This condition, in comparison to the past, made children even more vulnerable and made it more and more difficult for them to reach maturity and to participate in adult life.

Schools were built to house these children. To "raise them up right" and yet it seems that no one ever stopped to consider that for all of those previous centuries, such absurd constructs did not even exist.

Children became separated from their families. They were brought in and away from nature and they were segregated from adults. All of this happened because people were told that schools were necessary for children to learn.

> *"Don't pay attention to other people's minds. Look straight ahead, where nature is leading you – nature in general, through the things that happen to you; and your own nature, through your own actions."*
>
> *- Marcus Aurelius*

Van den Berg described Western society after World War II as "profoundly changed and manifesting an alarming degree of disorder and instability".

He perceived that: "We think differently and feel differently, we behave differently and dress differently. The relationships between man and woman, between adults and youth, as well as amongst adults and amongst youth show a fermenting unsettledness".

He astutely saw that, in such a time of great change and societal disorder, the influence of social and cultural factors on people's behavior, relationships and mental health in general needed to be understood and taken into account.

It has been over fifty years since he wrote his essay and we have moved even further yet.

7

HOW WE LEARN

But back to how we learn.... Another genius of our time, Albert Einstein said "I never teach my pupils, I only attempt to provide the conditions in which they can learn." In my experience and research, I've come to the conclusion that learning occurs naturally, but teaching isn't natural at all. If we look at what we call 'primitive' societies - there are no schools and no teaching. Yet, the people live so harmoniously and so successfully.

> *"Men are born ignorant, not stupid; they are made stupid by education."*
>
> *- Bertrand Russell*

The young ones are learning from the older children, the older children are learning from the adults, sometimes the adults are learning from the children and everyone is in awe and present when the elders share as they have spent the most time living, so they have amassed the most learning.

> *"I pay the schoolmaster, but it is the schoolboys who educate my son."*
>
> *- Ralph Waldo Emerson*

The interesting thing is that there is no one officially teaching. Everyone in the village is learning on their own initiative and all of the time, which is so powerful.

There is no pressure on what is learned and what has been missed because the consensus is that everyone will get just exactly what they need, and the beautiful thing is that they DO.

There is no need to augment this way of learning in any way. In fact, you can't really augment it even if you try, and we have tried, and it is not working.

Why? Because no matter how we build our institutions which hold children every day, there's no way you can make a child learn better than he would if he or she wants to. And that is because of the nature of learning itself – which is that children are learning all of the time.

Let me emphasize that – children are learning all of the time.

So, while you think your child is learning in school - yes, you are correct - but WHAT is it that the child is truly learning?

Is your child learning to stand in line, to shut up, to sit still, that he does not have a voice and does not matter? Is he learning that his time is not valuable? That his or her creations and ideas and input really do not matter? That there is a way one can act to pass, be accepted and be thought of as 'good'? Maybe he is learning to cheat or take out his aggression on the smaller ones, the weaker ones...

The rigidness of the environment of school itself actually stunts a child's intellectual growth because it retards it.

Yes, it slows it down, it dumbs it down.

This is because children are not given *the freedom to learn* in a way that is inherent to their natural drive and their human instincts. The ones we come wired with at birth, remember – the add-ons that come with the human package.

We have to understand and accept that learning is so much more than the acquisition of mass quantities of information. Education should strive to awaken the child's natural capabilities, and not educate.

If you really want to unmask the pretensions of compulsory education, then another book you have to read *Compulsory*

Mis-Education by Paul Goodman.

Paul lays it out and tells it as it is. He believes that school is 'another racket where people are taught they need the ministrations of the school system'.

This wonderful book was written in the sixties and is a bracing reminder that human beings are born free and possess the capacity to shape their own lives outside the institutionalized context of schooling.

Not only are your children born free. They should have the freedom to learn, as I mentioned above, inherent to their natural drive and human instincts. As a homeschool and unschooling parent, the only "job" I had as my child's teacher, was to instill in them a love of learning - which I confess, was really not that difficult since they came wired that way.

The ability to learn on their own makes it more likely that later, when these children are adults, they can continue to learn what they need to know to meet newly emerging needs, interests, and goals. I simply had to step out of my children's way and provide a space and the resources or tools they asked for − for their learning to happen.

In the words of John Holt, "If children are given access to enough of the world, they will see clearly enough what things are truly important to themselves and to others, and they will make for themselves a better path into that world than anyone else could make for them."

There is no way to fail at this, provided you have a genuine interest to adventure and explore with your child. (*This means going to the library, to places where a variety of things are happening which provide stimulation and information.*)

In other words, sitting at home doing nothing except starring at soap operas all day does not show evidence of having a genuine interest to adventure and explore. You do have to get out more and learn to ask questions.

Unschooling does not mean that it is a "hands off" approach. You do not just walk away. Yes, children are learning all of the time but you are there to facilitate and guide the process.

As a parent of an unschooled child, you have certain responsibilities to carry out. You need to provide resources, support, guidance, information, and advice to facilitate experiences that aid your children in accessing, navigating, and making sense of the world.

Examples of this includes the sharing interesting books, articles, and activities with your children, helping them find knowledgeable people to explore an interest with, anyone from physics professors to automotive mechanics, and helping them to set goals and to figure out what they need to do to meet those goals.

Teach them to question everything. Ask questions about everything with your child, even if you know the answers. And ask in the way your child would ask until the child learns through your modeling to ask this way himself.

(Actually, most 2 and 3 years old have this capability and it works quite well when they ask "but why is it this way?", "but why does it happen like this?", etc.)

Ask WHY of everyone who has anything of interest to offer. Ask the postman when you collect the mail "Why do some postmen carry a mailbag and walk door to door while others drive the mail truck?" Ask the produce man at the grocery store, "Why are the apples stacked and sorted according to their color?"

You will be surprised how many people, going about their day in a quiet way will be more than happy that you stopped them to ask and made something called conversation. See, humans are funny that way being social animals and all. We like to look into each other's eyes and hear each other's voices.

When we are given the opportunity to talk about what we do, we usually stand a bit taller and even appear to shine at times. Make friends with the postman, the garbage man, the grocery clerk, the vegetable man at the farmer's market. Talk to people.

Meet these people and be kind to them, see them as your children's teachers because they are and they are all around you all of the time.

Yes, I can hear the pessimists saying "people are busy, angry – my butcher is a jerk" or whatever...

My answer to this is:

1) Exercise your freedom of choice and find another or
2) Ask yourself, what can you do to help this persons' experience be a bit better?

In regards to your child's learning, trust that he is. My experience is that the parents question themselves more than their children because of their own experiences in school.

Know that you are on the right track when you are following your instincts, when your child is learning at his own pace and when you, the parent can stretch your imaginations to reach beyond the limits of a public school education.

Remind yourself that nature and our evolution is a natural process where as school is one which is a man-made construct, an idea someone had. A bad idea.

Okay, maybe a good idea at first, but an idea which has grown perverse and damaging and too far removed from serving the needs of children. We originally sent them to school to give them an opportunity for a better life. Today, they have an opportunity for a better life if they are left out of school.

School is not what we wanted to build. It has become an institution. A factory. A prison.

8

GRANDMOTHER'S TASTES

Now remember, it is human instinct to survive and to succeed. What is success? Is it the same for all of us? Is it monetary and materialistic or is it happiness and a sense of well-being? What if success is freedom - doing what you really want to do? And what if success is the pursuit of what our heart desires.....

> *"What we want to see is the child in pursuit of knowledge, not knowledge in pursuit of the child."*
> *- George Bernard Shaw*

The main question that parents should be asking themselves is "am I giving my child what he or she needs to successfully meet the challenges of this rapidly changing world?"

The fastest and most useful way to get to a place of true learning, I have found, is by immersion in the subject at hand. This may mean immersion for a week, a month or a year. Obviously in a very young child, it may also mean just a couple of hours... but to be a master of anything one has to be immersed fully.

I have a favorite Chinese proverb:

> *Tell me and I will forget*
> *Show me and I may remember*
> *Involve me and I will understand.*

Isn't that beautiful?

It is through being involved and a hands-on learning style, as in an apprenticeship - we retain the most and what really gives us the fullest understanding of any subject.

A quick proof of this is to look at yourself and your favorite activity, hobby, pastime or sport. I venture to guess that if you practice stamp collecting - you can tell me things about stamps that 99.9% of the population has no idea about. I venture to guess that a person listening to you speak passionately about stamps, they would assume you are an expert on the subject, a master. Pause for a moment and ask yourself why this is.

No one came along and "MADE" you study stamps, you just decided one day you liked to collect them and as you went about your days, discovering which were the most prized or unique or rare ones to collect you were gathering facts that you retained because the information really interested you.

This is because it is important to you, because it is useful to you in the realm of your stamp collecting and so you learned all of these wonderful things about stamps that most people really have no clue about, right?

How is that possible? Did it take you a semester, or a year or a 4 year time period for sitting 8 hours a day, 5 days a week to get that knowledge?

No. Because when you were focused on it you were perfectly immersed and therefore you retained that knowledge - because it had practical use and value for you. You learned quickly and the learning was easy, so easy you did not feel like you had to do much work to get it done.

Let's look at your neighbor. He may collect comic books or Elvis memorabilia. You know, he probably knows 99.9% of things about Elvis memorabilia or comic collecting that you never even knew.

Not only that – he most likely knows things that you did not even know that you did not know. Does that make sense?

He is acutely aware of things that a person who is not interested in comics or Elvis has no idea even exist - yet to his experience, it has practical use and value for him. And as he immerses himself in the quest for finding out more to build his collection, or add value to his collection – he is fully immersing himself, enough to master his subject.

Across the street lives a neighbor who has the hobby of knitting. Do you know that a knitter can tell you all about the different weights and materials in yarns, their origins, the history of yarns in textiles and so on for hours... and her husband is a sports fan, and he can tell you scores and plays all the way back from 1950. He knows the players' names and numbers, he knows their coaches and how they did at the playoffs, if they made it. He knows that this is the first time in 11 years that they got to do this or that.

He remembers where he was when he watched the game, who ran how many goals, etc. because he was immersed and it is what is practical and valuable to him. He can lecture all day to his wife, who knits, and she can appear to be listening intently as she knits - but how much of his interest will she retain?

Do you think she remembers the score some team had in 1960 - not likely - and by the same token, does he know the difference between mohair, wool, alpaca or other fibers? Does he even care? Does she?

Now what I just illustrated makes sense to most logical people. It is not rocket science, not does it take a genius to agree. And yet these same people expect their child to sit still and listen to other people's fragmented sound bites of information all day, every day for what seems as long as a lifetime.

They do not touch, smell, feel, live, breathe and experience most of these facts and bits of data. They have no relationship to them whatsoever - and yet we expect, no - we demand that they retain this information - one size fits all, for all children.

It's not fair.

It's not logical.

It's not right.

We don't consider the fact that the children are at different levels of development that they come from different socio-economic backgrounds, that they have different ways of learning and perceiving the world. We don't care that they have challenges and lives outside of the class, that they are growing and having their physical being change. We just take it as being par for the course that they go to school.

"Go to school!"

"Why?"

"Because I say so. Because you have to. Because that is the way that it is."

How they are supposed to learn this unnatural way and how truly absurd this idea of learning in this way does not even cross our minds. Yet millions of children are subject to this every day.

Force does not make for a love of anything. Compliance does not awaken any natural capabilities or talents except anger.

An interesting read I would like to mention at this juncture is a book called *Power Versus Force: The Hidden Determinants of Human Behavior* by Dr. David R Hawkins MD PhD.

Force is incomplete and needs energy, whereas power is total and complete requiring nothing outside and making no demands. Force consumes whereas power energizes. Power gives life and energy whereas force takes these away.

Power is associated with compassion and feeling positively about yourself whereas force involves judgment and makes us feel poorly about ourselves.

Learning is power. Schooling is force.

On my own journey, I have practiced the questioning stage so much with my children, that even now that they are grown, it is still with me...

Why? Why do we subject them to an environment that is not beneficial to their natural learning pattern?

Why? Are we too busy to notice, or worse - to care?

Why do we not even have the time anymore to sit and think about what is best for them and their needs?

Have we ourselves forgotten how to think?

Have we become incognizant?

"The individual mind is like a computer terminal connected to a giant database. The database is human consciousness itself, of which our own cognizance is merely an individual expression, but with its root in the common consciousness of all mankind. This database is the realm of genius; because to be human is to participate in the database, everyone, by virtue of their birth, has access to genius."

You know, I feel so blessed that now, after investing my time into my children, that I am privileged to witness some pretty amazing and awesome things. An example of this is my 22 year old son who has written several books. One of these is *Immersion Mastery.*

I did not expect him to write this.

I did not ask him to write this.

And he's written a book before, when he was only 10 years old. This is something inside of him and I honor that.

He wanted to be a Shaman and he learned with a friend, he asked to go on that journey and I allowed it. I encouraged him. He wanted to document it and that was how he wrote *My Journey To Becoming A Mayan Shaman* when he was ten years old.

He is now passionate about sharing what he lived, that is the greatness. Immersion is how he learned and he looks around and sees broken children who are crying for help, begging for help. They come to him, they seek him out and they ask him for help in making sense of all of the madness. And he guides them and shares alternative ways, and they are thankful.

He has coached them and guided them out of running away from home, getting into drugs, even talked them out of committing suicide.

So many children today are in crisis and they are not being heard. They come to my son as a guide, a light, a leader – and when I say leader, I have to refer to the words of John Holt...

"Leaders are not, as we are often led to think, people who go along with huge crowds following them. Leaders are people who go their own way without caring, or even looking to see, whether anyone is following them. 'Leadership qualities' are not the qualities that enable people to attract followers, but those that enable them to do without them.

They include, at the very least, courage, endurance, patience, humor, flexibility, resourcefulness, stubbornness, a keen sense of reality, and the ability to keep a cool and clear head, even when things are going badly. True leaders, in short, do not make people into followers, but into other leaders."

Those words come from a book called *Teach Your Own*. And this book was a prime influence in the way I allowed learning to dance in and around the lives of my own children.

It is there, for them to discover, court, challenge, enjoy, enliven, and be present with. It is as intimate and as personal as their own souls and being-ness.

It is **THEIRS** and I would never dream of taking their experience away and instead pushing upon them **MY** vision of the world or my experience.

And this happens in the most subtle ways...

Let me give you an example that will make my mother crazy if she ever reads this. (*Sorry mom!*)

So, my mother likes to eat and as she is eating, she enjoys vocalizing her experience. Some examples of her comments are "Mmmmm, this is so sweet" or "Oh, I cannot eat this, this is disgusting" or "Why do you eat that, it isn't sweet at all." and so on.

Many years ago, as she would express this way, I could see Zack look at the food and question himself eating it. But I let it slide... I am not sure the process was even conscious or if I really gave it any thought.

A few days or weeks later, we were at the table again and Zack said "I am not eating this Mama, it is disgusting".

Wow.

I never heard him say anything like that before. Especially about our food.

Note: do you notice these things in your child and actually pause to pay attention to how they happen?

I looked up from my food, shocked because I knew that it was one of his absolute favorites.

So I said "It is? I think I remember that you told me you liked this"

He answered "I know Mama, I did. But that was before Babi told me it was disgusting". (*Babi is 'grandma' in Czech*)

Interesting, isn't it? Did she set him aside and give him a dissertation on the disgusting-ness of this particular dish? Of course not. Did she secretly steal him away and then hypnotize him that the dish was disgusting? No.

This is a perfect example of how children learn all of the time. In this case, what did he learn? My mother did not have to test him on that or write it on the chalkboard. He got that lesson from her and she's not even a teacher.

Of course, I will share (*and confess*) that my poor mother then had the late night phone call with the lecture on how all people have different palettes and taste buds and how my children should all be allowed to formulate our own tastes and experiences at the dinner table and in relation to food, etc.

Long story short, I explained to her that if she wanted to ever have dinner with us again, that she needed to focus on using her mouth to chew her food instead of talking and thus 'poisoning all of us' with her taste buds or she would not be invited to come to dinner again.

Pretty extreme. I know, but that is how I roll as a Mama bear and that is my job as a parent. I need to be alert, aware, on guard. I need to make sure that my children are learning things that will benefit them and not harm them. In a home environment, I have this power. However, in school, this is completely out of my control.

Now… I can laugh at this now because it is quite extreme - but at the same time, if you think about it in the way I just

Kytka Hilmar-Jezek

explained - it's really not.

The power of his voice and his experience was my priority as his mother and his experience was being influenced by someone of a completely different chemical makeup, biology, etc.

How unfair was it to him that his own sense of taste be distorted in this way.

This is where and how learning happens, so we need to be aware and conscious of the process, how it works and then just create a space that provides the best environment and surroundings to facilitate the optimum learning experience.

This is also an example of what I call "going to bat for your child" and providing the fierce protection from potentially damaging influences.

I didn't know it then but I was working so hard on myself. I was dedicated and committed. I was in Olympic-like training to be the very best version of myself as a mother and then my mother would come as a guest for two hours and undo it with one sentence? It was unacceptable. If she wanted to come, she would have to at least be conscious of my efforts.

I laid down a line and I asked her not to cross it. I constructed a boundary. The reality is that you have to set boundaries. You have to be strong. That is just how it is when you are the parent and your child is the child. No excuses. No sleeping on the job.

No one ever said it would be easy and you signed up automatically the day you brought your child into the world,

You always have to go to bat for your child and be his or her voice, and they need to see you do that - in a kind and gentle way - but in this way they also learn that you truly want the best for them and that means to allow them to make their own choices. The "side effect" of this is that your child trusts you.

How powerful is that for you and for your child?

Trust and respect. When you have this with your child, you learn, stretch, expand and grow, too, right along you're your child. This does not just apply to a homeschooler or an unschooled child. This applies to every child.

All children are influenced all of the time and everywhere.

When your thinking shifts and you awaken to the journey of parenting in this way, then you start to study the environment and the people around you more closely. You develop an acute awareness. You become awake as a parent.

You begin to have thoughts like "maybe Chuck-e-Cheese is not the best place to have a birthday party"

You begin to question things.

"What values does this teach?"

Your mind goes even deeper and you begin to think about what a birthday actually represents.

A birthday is a celebration of ones birth. How do I want my child to experience our honoring for him and his coming into the world? By attempting to buy them with loads of materialistic things? By over stimulating them with a loud party or mechanical toys?

Your awareness becomes a guide. Your intuition begins to serve you. You develop a sense of knowing and this knowing guides you.

The gifts we share in our family are poems and letters that express our feelings and what we mean to one another. Believe it or not, that is perfectly enough. In fact, these are the treasures that we cherish.

I am not under pressure struggling to keep up with the Joneses to fill my child's room (*and head*) with material gadgets and things. They are not pressured to have the next best gadget to "fit in" anywhere. In fact, they do not care about any of the latest and greatest gadgets at all. They don't have a wish list, and if they did, I am sure gadgets would not be on it.

I work to get them any book, tool or resource they need and we usually find these at the library or through the community of friends we have, and we trade.

In this way, I honor their true being and essence, their presence, their very being each and every day and they do mine. In this way, we are a family with love and respect for one another, and we are also the best of friends. We actually LIKE to spend time together.

We enjoy each other's company. We are best friends.

It is not so difficult to have this.

Why does modern culture or society tell us this is impossible and that teenagers are terrible and they all hate their parents?

That is not my experience at all.

9

KIDS TO THE BACK

But let's get back to school. Let's talk about schooling in a rapidly changing world. Let's look at what happens to children when they are separated from the world and are only grouped with their peers.

Do they grow up and spend all of the time with a group of twenty other 25 year olds? How does that prepare them for real life, or the real world? Can they relate and socialize to people of all ages, from all walks of life?

Are they being taught how to relate to people of all ages in school? Because that is exactly what is waiting for them on the outside. A world filled with people of all backgrounds, all circumstances and all ages.

School socializes children. Really? I see a lot of pack mentality and peer pressure, but I am not seeing much more than that.

The reality is that if you put your personal beliefs and embedded values aside and you were to look at it from a purely logical standpoint, we could possibly even say that school is a form of segregation, and completely against a child's civil rights.

Ms. Rosa Parks does not have to sit on the back of the bus anymore but so why should our children have to sit in school?

Students are segregated by ability and achievement levels. They segregate students by age. They segregate children based on state mandated test results. Some kids are "gifted" and others are "slow learners".

When a child is in school the community consists of a same age peer group. The parent has little influence or knowledge of who this is. And while everyone speaks of how a child needs to go to school to become socialized, the exact opposite is what happens at school. This is because the conditions common in conventional schools, like age segregation, a low ratio of adults to children, a lack of contact with the community, a lack of people in professions other than teachers or school administration, an emphasis on the smarter children, shaming of the failing children, and an emphasis on sitting, create an unhealthy social environment.

All of that actually adds to de-socializing a child. It puts them into an artificial construct of reality. Pulled away from home and out of a normal reality of space and time, they are "saved by the bell" and put into the school matrix. (*I am being sarcastic here!*)

No one asks if they feel they are getting value there. They just have to go. In stark contrast, an unschooled child has the time to share a role in their greater community, therefore making them capable of relating more to both older as well as younger individuals and finding their place within more diverse groups of people.

Critics of unschooling argue that not being in school inhibits social development because the child has been removed from a 'ready-made peer group' of diverse individuals. (*The other kids trapped in the matrix.*)

Yet study after study shows that children not in school tend to be much more mature than their schooled peers. Obviously, this is a direct result of the wide range of people they have the opportunity to interact with on a day to day basis.

So which do you think serves them better in life?

I realize this sounds a bit harsh - but think about it? Wouldn't you agree that your child has a right to learn what interests him or her? Who are we, especially in this day and age of technology, to push ideas, systems and processes on our children which may be obsolete in just a few years?

Has anyone offered the students to test their teachers? To quiz the teachers on subjects that interest the students? What if the students were allowed to make the teachers stay at school during certain days and hours? Does that sound ridiculous again?

This invites yet a whole other opening to a whole new series of questions about so called "education" and schooling. I know this all sounds extreme, but please bear with me. My intention, remember, is to help you understand HOW CHILDREN LEARN.

Anytime there are forced mandates and segregation, it looks more like indoctrination than like education to me.

If you do the research and study the history, eventually you will come to realize that the true purpose of our public school system has more to do with control than it does with learning.

Once again, I ask you to read *The Underground History of American Education.*

If you have ever had an inkling that there may be something wrong with the public school system, this book explains it all fully in amazing encyclopedic detail. You will feel that you are reading a secret history that you were never supposed to find out about. Trust me. Read the book.

Research has shown that students are actually less intelligent, less self-reliant, less capable of genuine analytical and independent thought, and they are actually more conformist, and more easily controlled than children who are not schooled.

Yes.

Children who do not attend school show up being smarter than schooled children. Consistently.

This is because they are learning all of the time and they are not confined to the artificial construct of a classroom. The entire world becomes their classroom.

Unschooling students learn through their natural life experiences including play, household responsibilities, personal interests and curiosity, internships and work experience, travel, books, elective classes, family, mentors, and social interaction. This encourages exploration of activities initiated by the children themselves, believing that the more personal learning is, the more meaningful, well-understood and therefore useful it is to the child.

A fundamental premise of unschooling is that curiosity is innate and that children *want to learn.*

Therefore, the argument can be made that institutionalizing children in a so-called "one size fits all" or "factory model" school is an inefficient use of the children's time, because it requires each child to learn a specific subject matter in a particular manner, at a particular pace, and at a specific time regardless of that individual's present or future needs, interests, goals, or any preexisting knowledge he or she might have about the topic.

Education is not learning, and school is not a natural environment to gather what one needs to go forth in life and in the world.

> *"Education is a weapon, whose effect depends on who holds it in his hands and at whom it is aimed."*
>
> *- Joseph Stalin*

Did you note who wrote the quote above. Stalin!

From his book *How Children Fail,* John Holt writes: "We ask children to do for most of a day what few adults are able to do for even an hour. How many of us, attending, say, a lecture that doesn't interest us, can keep our minds from wandering? Hardly any." So before blindly accepting that schools are where kids go to learn, I suggest to parents please get educated and informed.

Do your own research and study. Ask the *why* questions. Who is your child's teacher? Do you get to choose? Of course not.

Parents of school children have little say regarding who their instructors and teachers are. But when your child is unschooled, you as the parent are obviously more involved in the selection of the coaches or mentors your child is working with and you know with whom they are build lasting and ongoing relationships.

Try to spend time with your child's teacher more than just at the parent teacher conference meeting (*which if you are in the corporate world is like the meetings at work where everyone has to make everything look good because the bigwigs are coming!*)

Do you just trust that the person is a good person, worthy of modeling? Because by default, remember, your child is actively taking the authority of these people and believing it and not only that, he is internalizing it. Not only what they are teaching, but the character of that person; their gestures, their mannerisms, parts of their personality.

Critics of unschooling see this as an extreme educational philosophy, with concerns that unschooled children will lack the social skills, structure, and motivation of their peers, while proponents of unschooling say exactly the opposite is true: self-directed education in a natural environment better equips a child to handle the "real world."

Where do you stand? Do you believe that children are learning all of the time? Do you worry about who your child's teacher is, who his peers are and what he does all day in school?

Because remember that whatever your child is exposed to will become a part of the basic feelings that he will have about his sense of self.

Can you even walk into a school anymore and walk with your child all the way to class or do they not allow parents past security these days? Security at schools?

Yes. It is terrifying. Iron gates, large fences, metal detectors. All of this in the world of childhood? Doesn't something inside of you instinct want to say "what's wrong with this picture?"

Have our children been reduced to chattel; to numbers, to faceless names in a book? In school, I believe they have.

So again, I urge you to PLEASE study *The Underground History of American Education.*

In fact, read all of the books by John Taylor Gatto. You can justify hours and hours spent watching a ridiculous television program or a movie, why not commit yourself to sift through some of the material I recommend and get the information you need to make an informed decision which concerns your child's life.

Gatto has authored numerous books on education and has nearly 30 years' experience in the classroom. Again, if you have not heard of him, you should. He was named New York City Teacher of the Year in 1989, 1990, and 1991. He was also named New York State Teacher of the Year in 1991.

In 1991, he wrote a letter announcing his retirement, titled "*I Quit, I Think*" to the op-ed pages of the Wall Street Journal, saying that he no longer wished to "hurt kids to make a living."

He no longer wanted to HURT KIDS. He believed that as a public school teacher, that is exactly what he was doing.

He then began a public speaking and writing career, and has received several awards including the Alexis de Tocqueville Award for Excellence in Advancement of Educational Freedom in 1997. Now I'll quote:

> *"These institutions that produce barely literate, dependent, conformist, incomplete individuals full of emotional and psychological problems, who lack real knowledge (and whose capacity for acquiring such is deliberately weakened or eliminated), and who are just educated' enough to pay their taxes and buy the latest products, are not, in fact, failing schools - on the contrary, they are performing their designated function PERFECTLY. That purpose is to mold people in such a way as to make them more easily controlled by the corporations and the state."*

The above comes from a review of the book entitled *The Underground History of American Education: A School Teacher's Intimate Investigation Into the Problem of Modern Schooling.*

Get the book. Get it today. Get it at any cost. Get it because your child deserves the best. Get it because you deserve to know the truth.

"When someone considers himself to be totally governed by influences outside himself, he sits in apathy".

- Ruth Minshull

Let's review the definition of apathy (*Noted from The American Heritage Dictionary*):

1. Lack of emotion or feeling.
2. Lack of interest in things generally found exciting, interesting, or moving; indifference.

What do such things say about the institution of school? Do we have schools overflowing with apathetic children? Are these the children who bully and terrorize one another? Do we have shocking statistics of child suicide? Do we have child killers going into the schools on mass killing sprees?

Yes, we do.

Now again – this is highly sensitive to many people, especially if you have children in school. But please continue - putting your head in the sand like an ostrich does not solve anything.

"The suicide rate among preteen and young teen girls spiked 76 percent, a disturbing sign that federal health officials say they can't fully explain. For all young people between ages 10 to 24, the suicide rate rose 8 percent from 2003 to 2004 - the biggest single-year bump in 15 years - in what one official called "a dramatic and huge increase."

- Associated Press

From Healthy Place: America's Mental Health Channel: "Many people have thought that the main reason that children and adolescents try to kill themselves is to manipulate others or get attention or as a 'cry for help'. However, when children and adolescents are actually asked right after their suicide attempts, their reasons for trying suicide are more like adults. For a third, their main reason for trying to kill themselves is they wanted to die. Another third wanted to escape from a hopeless situation or a horrible state of mind. Only about 10% were trying to get attention. The children who truly wanted to die were more depressed, angrier, and were more perfectionistic."

In other words – they were not good enough in their minds. Their self-esteem and self-worth was incredibly low. They could not make the grade. They *wanted to die.*

> *"How could youths better learn to live than by at once trying the experiment of living?"*
>
> *- Henry David Thoreau*

At this age, the pressures they have can only come from two places, in the home or in the school.

Is there any circumstance or condition where any child should ever be made to feel like they want to die? Especially when it is human instinct to LIVE and LIVE WELL?

10

SEEKING ANSWERS

I share all of this because we need information to make wise decisions and the best decisions, even when best may not be the most convenient or the most popular.

Before parents want to shrug off the concept of teaching their own child, in whatever form that may take, I recommend they do the research and gain a true understanding of the facts behind how children truly learn and the damaging psychology that is imprinted by the school environment.

Reading the materials I recommended by John Taylor Gatto and John Holt is a wonderful way to get more acquainted with how children actually learn.

Once you understand that process, you begin thinking about alternatives. A recommended book for this is *Instead of Education: Ways to Help People do Things Better* - which is also a wonderful read.

You see, the resources are all there. All that waits is your action to seek them out. And whether the reason you take the next step is out of fear or to move towards something better – use whatever means will push you to the next level.

I rarely ever refer to the Bible or any other spiritual texts, but in this case I will refer to the Bible which tells us:

> *"Ask, and it shall be given you; seek, and ye shall find; knock, and it shall be opened unto you. For every one that asketh*

receiveth; and he that seeketh findeth; and to him that knocketh
it shall be opened."

The Bible is written on the premise that God created man-kind to seek. And I do agree that mankind is seeking, and learning, all of the time.

Whether it is an intuition, another sad story in the news, a tragedy in your community or just a feeling of disconnect and loss of what your hopes and dreams were when you were just anticipating having a child – I invite you to seek the answers.

Van der Berg wrote: "Our children are late in everything. They no longer fit the institutions founded for them. In particular they have difficulties in adjusting themselves to school; they have become too immature for it. We usually blame the school, which we are inclined to consider an old fashioned institution. But the way school now functions is additional evidence of the misunderstanding between young and old. School is in need of a renovation; not a change of nonessentials or of parts, but a renewal of the whole thing. Education as a whole has to be revised; and if the revision is to be effective, it must be nothing less than a total renewal of educational methods, which - as the recent serious attempts at renewal indicate - will be so radical that the slightly older teachers will observe these changes with wonder and will not feel at home with them, even if they do not doubt their necessity and agree as to their effectiveness. For it is clear to anyone who has anything to do with children and with education that something has to happen. Ever more children are experiencing serious difficulties during the first few years of primary school. Ever more children remain apart from what is being taught during a good part of the years they go to primary school.

Schools are haunted by the ghost called alexia, one of the family of ghosts to which infantile autism also belongs. It is quite clear that this situation cannot be allowed to continue."

Note: Alexia (from Greek (a-), meaning "absence of, without", and (lexis), meaning "word") is a brain disorder in which a person is unable to understand written words. It refers specifically to the loss, usually in adulthood, of a previous ability to read.

William Feather wrote:

"Education is knowing where to go to find out what you need to know; and its knowing how to use the information you get."

This is why I am giving you this information today.

11

NEW PARADIGM

So what are the alternatives to school? If you have been reading this, then you know that no school is the best school in my opinion. But other alternatives do exist. They are homeschooling, unschooling, hackschooling, free schools, democratic schools, Sudbury schools, Waldorf schools and numerous more.

At least there are alternatives. Isn't it better to make an informed decision rather than just blindly following the crowd?

Ask yourself "what is the best way I can provide my child with an education that will prepare him or her for the world?" and go from there. Depending on your personal situation, economics, etc. you will have to make a choice based on your circumstance.

> *"Learning is the beginning of wealth. Learning is the beginning of health. Learning is the beginning of spirituality. Searching and learning is where the miracle process all begins."*
>
> *- Jim Rohn*

Learning is a natural instinct that belongs to the person who is doing it. It is a blessing and a birth right. It is meant to be formulated by the user, and just as each human is unique, so are the lessons and the learning which comes. You cannot force someone to learn something as much as you cannot make the horse drink water, even when you lead him to it.

`They have to think for themselves to make the knowledge their own and it benefits them on so many different levels when they do learn on their own. And by the way, when did we get so sure of ourselves to insist that we know better? Especially when the great minds and thinkers of the past *explicitly warn us* against this?

Great minds like Albert Einstein who said: "The only thing that interferes with my learning is my education." Or Peter Drucker who said: "We now accept the fact that learning is a lifelong process of keeping abreast of change. And the most pressing task is to teach people how to learn."

And "When a subject becomes totally obsolete we make it a required course." Or finally, one of my favorites from Tagore "Don't limit a child to your own learning, for he was born in another time."

Quotes are like modern day super condensed sound bites of wisdom that we can reflect upon and allow our mind the stretching exercise of pondering their meaning.

I have included many very inspirational and empowering quotes at the end of this book. I carried them written in a notebook in my purse. When I would feel myself slipping into status quo, I would consult with my oracle quotes (what I affectionately called them) and immediately I would be brought back to my center and strength. I urge you to read them, consider them and apply some of their wisdom in your lives.

"I always like to learn, but I don't always like to be taught."

- Winston Churchill

In his book *Learning All the Time,* John Holt writes:

"A child only pours herself into a little funnel or into a little box when she's afraid of the world - when she's been defeated. But when a child is doing something she's passionately inter-

ested in, she grows like a tree - in all directions.
THIS is how children learn, how children grow.
They send down a taproot like a tree in dry soil.
The tree may be stunted, but it sends out these roots, and
suddenly one of these little taproots goes down and strikes a
source of water. And the whole tree grows."

Isn't that beautiful?

How awesome is it to just accept that as a truth and let go of all of the other crap, that is really fairly new and unproven anyhow – except, when you truly delve and research, proven to be damaging to true learning.

This is the new paradigm. Everything is changing! You cannot deny that the world is changing at such a fast pace and that what the children learn this year is already becoming outdated next year.

The children who are allowed freedom to pursue their own interests *(also known as the "rebels and troublemakers")* are creating the business structures of this new paradigm.

You know who I am talking about. Steve Jobs, Richard Branson… They are becoming increasingly influential with the Internet providing a platform never seen before.

Most of our social media technology has been built by young entrepreneurs. Corporations are now seeking out these kids who have created viral YouTube videos and hiring them as consultants to their companies.

They are literally firing traditionally educated people with advanced degrees and looking to the youth to solve problems, create new technologies, etc.

School is "old school". The future is upon us.

> *"In times of change, learners inherit the earth, while the learned find themselves beautifully equipped to deal with a world that no longer exists."*
>
> *- Eric Hoffer*

It appears that Eric knew what was coming...

The systems that were created are now archaic and broken. We now have sick schools; places that resemble more of a prison than a school. As our educational process becomes increasingly irrelevant and more kids get lost in the shuffle to be scooped up by gangs/police, this book becomes all the more meaningful.

Schools have become toxic places where children are not even allowed to question and are expected to sit in passive acceptance of all that is presented as truth and world view.

We don't need no education
We don't need no thought control
No dark sarcasm in the classroom
Teachers leave them kids alone
Hey teacher leave them kids alone

- Another Brick In The Wall, Pink Floyd

The experience of school today is a very interesting precursor of what is happening today to our families with children, the way we raise our children, and the difficulty of the children in becoming productive adults.

Peter Block said "Good questions work on us, we don't work on them. They are not a project to be completed but a doorway opening onto greater depth of understanding, actions that will take us into being more fully alive."

But we are not taught to ask these questions that open doorways to greater depths of understanding.

We are instead forced to conform to a state controlled protocol and series of standardized tests. And just getting to that environment instills in us the fear that we may never experience such a doorway to take us into being fully alive. Because when did we ever imagine metal detectors, shootings, high fences and lock downs around any place for children?

Why has society grown so restless, aggressive and bullying?

Does building more secure schools solve this?

I think not. And what is next? Bigger prisons instead of universities? If that sounds extreme then here is your wakeup call – we are already there. Yes...

Did you know that America incarcerates more citizens by total number and more citizens by a percentage of the total than any other country on earth? We have 5% of the world's total population and 25% of the world's total prison population.

According to the Justice Policy Institute funding to build prisons has a direct impact on education. From 1984 to 1994, the state of California built 21 prisons and increased prison funding by 209 percent. In that same period, California built only one state university and increased university funding by only 15 percent. Numbers do not lie.

So, let's pretend that we (finally) agree that the school system is broken. Let's just pretend that we can wrap our heads around that for a moment. Would you agree that society itself has become schooled? That like Ivan Illich writes, it "costs the same to school both the rich and the poor in the same 'dependency'."

What are they really teaching? Do we even know what teaching is?

> *"But, good gracious, you've got to educate him first. You can't expect a boy to be vicious till he's been to a good school."*
>
> *- H. H. Munro*

Play along... this is just a book and only my opinion. I confess, as a radical home and unschooler, I do have a certain slant in my opinion, but that is based upon my own personal experience and research.

To come to your own conclusion, and make a truly informed decision, I am simply suggesting that you consider what I am sharing here, even if for a moment...

Who needs help? The children, right? WRONG. The parents. Consider that the parents may be as sick as the schools they force their children to serve their sentences in. Shocking?

Maybe.

> 'The pupil is thereby schooled to confuse teaching with learning, grade advancement with education, a diploma with competence and fluency with the ability to say something new. His imagination is schooled to accept service in a place of value. Medical treatment is mistaken for health care, social work for the improvement of community life, police protection for safety, military poise for national security, the rat race for productive work. Health, learning, dignity, independence and creative endeavor are defined as little more than the performance of the institutions which claim to serve these ends, and their improvement is made to depend on allocating more resources to the management of hospitals, schools and other agencies in question.'
>
> *- Ivan Illich*

School is the child's introduction to just one of the corporate/state bureaucratic agencies; ones which include the army, the media, the consumer society, the party and the church.

I know that is pushing buttons right now...

Breathe, take a sip of water, be brave and allow yourself to at least consider it. There are solutions and they will benefit not only your child, but you, too.

You are the one who has to first accept that what you have been told is a lie. Because until you do that, this will sound too radical. But I know you agree. Your child's classroom and school look and feel NOTHING like the classroom and school you remember.

It's okay. The school is broken. Not you. You are only as broken if you refuse to see it.

The world is changing... Maybe reading this is your invitation to join.

12

HOME OR UNSCHOOLING

"You learn at your best when you have something you care about and can get pleasure in being engaged in."
- Howard Gardner

What interests you? What interests your child? Do you regularly check in with each other and share? I had this profound insight when I gave birth to my son and it was that from this point forward I would have to be the best version of myself because I knew he was watching. Knowing this, I had this burning desire to model only the best qualities that were, until then, pretty dormant - spiritual qualities; unconditional love, forgiveness, patience, mindfulness, presence.

The miracle and blessing in this was that while I felt I was doing this for him, it was an incredible gift for me as a human being as well. The transformation to motherhood awakened in me a personal growth and spiritual journey that continues to this day. Being a parent has made me a much better human being and there is a very deep satisfaction in that. A deep sense of wealth that I had never experienced before...

As I have walked this path for 20 or so years, I can confidently share that a new paradigm is emerging and as guardians of the children, it is the parents that must be educated, mentored, informed, nurtured and supported.

Because this way of learning all of the time is truly reciprocal - we learn together, drawing out the very best in each other and forming a very strong bond built upon trust and a deep mutual respect. This in turn builds confidence, self-esteem and feelings of immense worth, on parent and child.

There is a sense of belonging, of being a part of something bigger than just oneself - that then is a natural seed for compassion, patience and understanding and having the skill to see obstacles and challenges as opportunities for even further learning and growth, further expansion.

Carol Ann Tomlinson, author of '*The Differentiated Classroom*' wrote:

> "*It is not so important to have all the answers as to be hungry for them.*"

So you may be wondering what the difference is between homeschooling and unschooling? In homeschooling the parents make decisions on how to best educate the child, while in unschooling the child makes those decisions for herself.

Unschooling means learning what one wants, when one wants, in the way one wants, for one's own reasons. The choice and control reside within the learner ... the child may find outside help in the form of parents, mentors, books, or formal lessons, but he or she is the one making the decisions about how best to proceed. Unschooling is trusting that your children are at least as clever and as capable as you are yourself.

In the book *Teach Your Own* John Holt writes: "I have used the words "home schooling" to describe the process by which children grow and learn in the world without going, or going very much, to schools, because those words are familiar and quickly understood. But in one very important sense they are misleading. What is most important and valuable about the home as a base for children's growth in the word is not that it is a better school than the schools but that it isn't a school at all."

Children are amazing and those who are allowed to design their own way of learning come up with some incredible alternatives.

They are brilliant, if given the chance to show it.

Let's take a look at *Hackschooling* and listen to Logan LaPlant: "I'm not tied to one particular curriculum, and I'm not dedicated to one particular approach. I hack my education. I take advantages of opportunities in my community and through a network of my friends and family. I take advantage of opportunities to experience what I'm learning, and I'm not afraid to look for shortcuts or hacks to get a better, faster result. It's like a remix or a mashup of learning. ... And here's the cool part: because it's a mindset, not a system, hackschooling can be used by anyone, even traditional schools."

Screen shot source: Makezine.com

And why does he call it "hackschooling"?

"A lot of people think of hackers as geeky computer nerds who live in their parents' basement and spread computer viruses, but I don't see it that way. Hackers are innovators. Hacker are people who challenge and change the systems to make them work differently, to make them work better. It's just how they think, it's a mindset. I'm growing up in a world that needs more people with the hacker mindset, and not just for technology. Everything is up for being hacked, even skiing, even education. So whether it's Steve Jobs, Mark Zuckerberg, or Shane McConkey, having the hacker mindset can change the world."

Keep in mind that Logan is only 13 years old.

And finally, we see right here what is important to Logan at 13 and I am sure will be equally important when he is 30, 40, 60 or 80: "We don't seem to make how to be healthy and happy a priority in our schools; it's separate from schools, and for some kids it doesn't exist at all, but what if we didn't make it separate? What if we based our education on the practice of being happy and healthy because that's what it is: a practice, and a simple practice at that? Education is important, but why is being happy and healthy not considered education? I just don't get it."

You can watch Logan LaPlant's Ted Talk in full and learn more about him on the Tedx University of Nevada page.

Of course Logan also pays homage to Sir Ken Robinson's famous 2006 TED talk on "*How Schools Kill Creativity*" saying that creativity is as important as literacy and should be treated with the same status. Thus, according to Logan, the key components of hackschooling are to be healthy, happy, and creative, with a hacker mindset.

Children today are different. Much different. The culture has changed. The technology has changed. It's time for schools to change, too. And as parents, until they change, we should exercise our freedoms to teach our own.

I understand you may believe your circumstance cannot allow it, but perhaps you have just not done enough research. Have you considered forming a co-op or sharing the plan with other parents? You could create your own smaller "classes" where children can be encouraged to get together and work on things that are of interest to all of them.

The mind is like a parachute, it only works when open and this book is an invitation to open your mind.

For the most part, I personally believe that we have lost trust in our own essential nature. We don't just mistrust children, we mistrust ourselves. We mistrust human nature itself.

"It is among the commonplaces of education that we often first cut off the living room and then try to replace its natural functions by artificial means. Thus we suppress the child's curiosity and then when he lacks a natural interest in learning he is offered special coaching for his scholastic difficulties."

- Alice Duer Miller

Mistrust is formed when a baby's needs go unmet, when a child is not seen or heard. Society is unpleasant, dangerous, unhappy, alienated, and unstable because in childhood our very human nature — being confident, joyous and loving — has been undermined and we simply live the way we are expected to.

What we believe is what we make our experience into. And what we believe is what we have been taught to believe by our parents and our experiences in school and in mainstream culture.

But again, consider this: what if what we have been told is wrong? What if we are brave enough to awaken to the truth that we have blindly been following and trusting in a system that maybe does not have our best interest at heart?

What if we make a conscious decision to trust ourselves and our children once more and we create the time and the place to put that into practice?

"What makes people smart, curious, alert, observant, competent, confident, resourceful, persistent - in the broadest and best sense, intelligent- is not having access to more and more learning places, resources, and specialists, but being able in their lives to do a wide variety of interesting things that matter, things that challenge their ingenuity, skill, and judgment, and that make an obvious difference in their lives and the lives of people around them."

- John Holt, Teach Your Own

What if we made a decision to give our children the freedom to find their own way? What if we allowed our child to shine like Logan LaPlant's parents?

Let's take it even further than that and make it not just in regards to school, but in regards to their life twenty-four hours a day.

What if I was to suggest that you never do anything for a child that it can possibly do for itself, even if it takes a while longer?

Yes, I know you are in a hurry - but what if this is a lesson for you to stop, to pause - to learn patience and to just wait. Will the world really fall apart? Is the world more important than your child, or is your child the world?

What you may not have considered is that when most parents take the quick fix and do it for the child quickly, just to get out the door - not only do you give the child the message that he's inefficient or incompetent, but you're actually preventing him from learning in that moment. You are preventing him from having faith in his own ability to accomplish and figure things out.

What if you take 5 minutes here and 5 minutes there and let him figure it out. This is true quality time, not the superficial play date on Sunday afternoon.

The goal is to trust the process and to slowly re-build mutual trust and respect, not only for one another, but for each other's journey and very personal experience. This is not only beneficial for the education process, but also for the family unit as well.

Give your child the message from the very beginning that you expect him to figure things out for himself. This grows a self-reliant and independent human being, one who is secure in himself, no matter what is going on in the world around him.

I rarely did anything for any of my children. Not because I was a lazy mother but because I did the necessary research and I understood how I was actually damaging them when I did want to do for them. I was interfering with their natural process, so I got out of the way.

You should get out of the way too.

I discovered that I didn't need to empower my children to trust their own nature. The tendency to trust is there, we are born that way. As parents, we just need to feel that we have been given the permission to step out of the way and simply allow it, allow the children to BE.

By trying to fill the child with everything, we empty him of so much of what he was born with...

Let's stop this. Let's stop this damage and abuse right now. It's okay to let it go. It was the old way, we didn't know any better. We believed we were doing the best for our child.

Acknowledge the intention. Say out loud, "I was doing the best for my child with the information I had at the time."

Take it a step further and state "I now have more information, so I will make the necessary decisions based on those choices to better serve my child, and to grow with him in the process." And forgive yourself and/or whomever your deep inner wounded one may want to blame for anything.

Holding onto that also no longer serves..."I release the blame... I forgive you, I free you and I free myself as I close that chapter and open a new chapter on my journey of parenting alongside my child."

We come to experience a profound unconditional love not by finding the perfection in a child, but by seeing them perfectly as they are.

- Kytka

It really IS that easy. Make the decision.

Living IS learning and when kids are allowed to live and experience fully and energetically and happily they are learning a lot, even if we don't always know what it is.

Let go of the need to measure their progress. Do we measure how many steps they are taking now as opposed to when they were only at 2 steps a day? The very idea of grading and measuring, when looked at in this context is totally absurd.

Stop the need to measure and to compare. Your child is a unique being, a one of a kind, the one and only, an original. Understand that and own it.

And the truth of human nature and nature itself always prevails – instinct and LIFE always wants to survive. When you truly accept that as your new belief then the Universe will show up to confirm it in so many ways.

As I was gathering my notes to prepare for this, I read that the woman behind the "No Child Left Behind" initiative is now saying publicly it does not serve students, teachers, or schools. The article was entitled "*Standardized Testing: The Monster That Ate American Education*".

Educational historian Diane Ravitch wrote: "If we think about what our needs are for the twenty-first century, and not just how do we compete in the world but how do we live in the world, how do we survive in the world - we need a generation of people who will succeed us who are thoughtful, who can reflect, who can think."

"Who can think."

That is the generation we need, not those who have learned to memorize just to pass.

Again, I need to pull forth from John Holt because no one expresses more elegantly how children learn then he does.

> "*The child is curious. He wants to make sense out of things, find out how things work, gain competence and control over himself and his environment, and do what he can see other people doing. He is open, perceptive, and experimental. He does not merely observe the world around him, He does not shut himself off from the strange, complicated world around him, but tastes it, touches it, hefts it, bends it, breaks it. To find out how reality works, he works on it. He is bold. He is not afraid of making mistakes. And he is patient. He can tolerate an extraordinary amount of uncertainty, confusion, ignorance, and suspense ...*

School is not a place that gives much time, or opportunity, or reward, for this kind of thinking and learning."

Very powerful.

Re-read it and allow the wisdom to really sink in.

John wrote these words in 1964, the year I was born. That was 50 years ago. This was before schools were in the crisis that they are in now.

His wisdom and his advice is even more valuable now. We live in an amazing time. Quantum Physics tells us that we are creating our reality and the world as we go, as we imagine it to be along the way.

So are you imagining the best version of yourself and of your child? What children need is not new and better curricula but access to more and more of the real world. They need plenty of time and space to think over their experiences, and to use fantasy and play to make meaning out of them. They need advice, road maps, guidebooks, to make it easier for them to get where they want to go - *not where we think they ought to go* - and to find out what they want to find out.

Children are born with a powerful desire to learn. Everything we do as parents and teachers must ensure that this powerful desire is kept alive. If there were to be one thing to be continually assessed it should be this desire.

Too many children leave with too little to show for their time at school. Too many leave alienated and powerless. Too many leave unprepared for the real world and we are living in a world where this is a massive handicap, because they need those skills now more than ever.

We do not know what changes are coming, and we are too old and rigid and stuck in our ways to even be able to make a healthy prediction...

It's not our time, and yet we cling, filling them up with our outdated ideals. Or not even our ideas but the old and outdated, regurgitated ideas that our own parents filled us with.

Let Go. This is THEIR TIME. The children are energized and ready. This is their time. Get out of their way.

Get. Out. Of. Their. Way!

It's their turn, their path, time for their glory and experience. Be present, be on standby to provide resources and open doors for them. This is the new paradigm parent. Let it be you.

Let's shift from owning our children to owning enough strength within ourselves to trust enough to let them go. And this implies to them that they can do it, and because of this, they will.

Speak to them as the leaders and visionaries that they are. Treat them as Ambassadors here, in the world we created, and invite them to improve it and better it. Invite them to make it their world.

It's their turn.

13

LIVING AND LEARNING

Dorothy Law Nolte wrote *Children Learn what They Live* in 1954 and I want to share it with you, to remind you the importance of being aware and present, because remember they are learning all of the time. The poem follows, but the entire book actually has some wonderful information on each of the values.

Children Learn What They Live

If children live with criticism, they learn to condemn.
If children live with hostility, they learn to fight.
If children live with fear, they learn to be apprehensive.
If children live with pity, they learn to feel sorry for themselves.
If children live with ridicule, they learn to feel shy.
If children live with jealousy, they learn to feel envy.
If children live with shame, they learn to feel guilty.
If children live with encouragement, they learn confidence.
If children live with tolerance, they learn patience.
If children live with praise, they learn appreciation.
If children live with acceptance, they learn to love.
If children live with approval, they learn to like themselves.
If children live with recognition, they learn it is good to have a goal.
If children live with sharing, they learn generosity.

If children live with honesty, they learn truthfulness.
If children live with fairness, they learn justice.
If children live with kindness and consideration, they
learn respect.
If children live with security, they learn to have faith in
themselves and in those about them.
If children live with friendliness, they learn the world is a
nice place in which to live.

Your children live with you and whatever you deliver to them.

They live in your trust that you will give them the best of yourself. They live in the confidence that the decisions you make on their behalf are ones which will best serve them in their adult lives.

The question is, are you fully aware and conscious of this at all times? Who do you need to become so that your children are learning the best of the world.

Do you recognize the profound gift that they bring and offer to you? Are you conscious and mindful of their presence, their gift to you? Are you in a place of profound gratitude that these wonderfully sentient beings came here at this time, and chose you as their guardian with an invitation to pull your from where you are stuck with an invitation to remind you to play more because that is when you grow best?

Knowing this how can you ever again speak to your child in a patronizing way?

Implying that they are not enough - not smart enough, not big enough, not good enough, not fast enough of whatever.

*They are capable and wonderful and wired
with all they need.
All they seek from you is unconditional
love and closeness.*

But the world need not center on them. Ignoring them at play actually makes them feel calm inside because they know you trust them to be safe or careful, so they are.

Do not patronize and say "do you want me to help you with that?"

I literally cringe when I see people take over their children's play. The child instantly looks so frustrated, angry and quickly appears bored. If you came and began to tell me how to do my work, I would feel the exact same way.

Wouldn't you?

Do you want me to come to you and tell you how to do your job? Leave your children alone and you will learn that when you do, they will practice and play and eventually invite you to join them.

Allow them the respect or leaving them to their very important and natural *work of play*. Note that I emphasized WORK OF PLAY - because it IS important. It is of the utmost importance as they are growing - it is children's work.

`We used to believe that school will teach them more than play will. The concept is absurd.

Remember Einstein's words. The man was a modern day genius:

> *"The only thing that interferes with my learning is my education."*

Try your best to never do anything to a child that will make him feel badly about himself.

Most people only understand that on the extreme level and they think "this doesn't apply to me". Yet many of us do this unconsciously, and we do it often. We do it with words and we do it with looks.

Sadly, if you watch parents interacting with their children you'll see that there are two predominant ways of interacting.

One is permissive:

"That's fine Jimmy, mommy knows it was an accident."

No consequence, no responsibility.

The other one is the punishing and blaming: "Didn't I tell you you'd break it? Your hands are too small to handle that, this is what always happens".

In today's culture, most people believe that these are "normal" ways to speak to a child. It is as if we don't know any other way.

But there is another way and you have been awakened to it today, reading this far, by hanging in there with me and by being open to a new and better way. So I commend you for that. I congratulate you. I respect and admire YOU!

The solution I found works best in communicating with children is in the form of information and natural consequences. The same way I would communicate with another adult. I don't separate "adult talk" and "child talk".

I speak "human to human" talk and I invite you to try it too.

Children are innately social; they want and crave information, so give it to them as you would to another adult, a fellow human being. Explain things as you would to a co-worker or a friend.

Do not blame and do not praise because both are just as insulting to the child and just as damaging to their forming sense of self. Just let them know.

If it involves a natural consequence - then let it happen. Trust me, if they have to deal with the consequence, they will learn from that experience and will be highly unlikely to repeat it.

And finally, live it. Walk your talk. This is not sometime, or part time, or quality time, this is *all the time.*

Do not go into overwhelm with "I barely have time as it is now" but rather look at how you can become a family once again; breakfast time, dinner time, outings and errands together. Explore and have adventures together and ask the "WHY" again and again everywhere you go.

Commit to it now. State it out loud.

"I commit to try to befriend my child and to hang out with him or her."

Yes, I said hang out with — like you would with your friends.

Stop the madness of segregation and separation. Children are as human as you are — they can go where you go, and they should!

I have always taken my children to workshops, seminars, events, the theater, opera and museums. Avoid the specific "children's days" with a lot of children running amok as they go through with their teacher. Instead, go on a weekday. Take the day off. You'll have the museum to yourselves.

Enjoy each other's company. Become friends. LIKE each other and love UNCONDITIONALLY.

Check in with yourself and make sure that you are being a clear model and then there's no conflict. This means that you need to work on being a bit more mindful of your actions. Perhaps you have slacked a bit... that is okay.

It's time to get back in gear. It's time to take action. It's time to set a new course and charter new waters....

Nature designed us to learn and to grow and usually, we not only stay safe — we blossom and thrive when doing so. Yes, grownups too! We are *all* learning all of the time. I am confident that you learned something by reading this.

It's not scary outside of the box — it's freeing, it's expressive, it's joyous and you can breathe again.

So I invite you to climb out of the box and come play. Pull your child out of the box and create an adventure together.

Sit together and discuss ideas and map out some plans, some suggestions and together, as a family unit — formulate a new paradigm blueprint of what you want your life to look like.

Create a family vision board and commit to it, and day by day, take small baby step efforts in that direction. Let your family know that you have had an insight, a vision of a better way and you want their help to make this new family dream for you all a reality. Elicit their help.

If you expect children to do the right thing, they most always do. If you ask their help, they most always want to help.

I know that if you are struggling with overwhelm that you do not know where to begin, that you lack a support system, that it may be too much for you or even that deep down, you are so disconnected from your child that you truly have no idea how to even begin to relate to them, but ask the Universe.

Voice it out loud. Get comfortable voicing it and then voice it to your other family members.

I am asking you to rise to this challenge because I know that there is light on the other side of this, which is really just a fear of the unknown.

I counsel families and they have all been at this place, and this is the hardest place to be because of the fear of the unknown. But the other side is what you want.

You can build it.

It will come manifest....

I ask you to look to the Source and ask for the strength to overcome any fears and take the chance. I ask that whenever you go into overwhelm, that you chunk it down into little baby steps. You will be surprised. It will be easier than you think.

Imagine how your life will look six months from now, a year from now, five years from now. How will it look if this information I have been sharing here today is implemented and works for you, too.

Imagine your relationship with your child one year from now. Are you now in the relationship with your child that you imagined you would have before he or she was born?

How wonderful would that be? You know, we all feel it, don't we? `We all feel that time is speeding up.

One year from now will be here sooner than you think, so focus on one day at a time, one small step for man – one giant step for all mankind.

And yes, you will have to sacrifice some things.

Good...

Purge.

Let go of things that no longer serve. Let go of the baggage.

Let go of the beliefs that do not serve. Release them. And slow down too.

Enough is enough.

It's time to slow down a bit and reconnect, recharge, rebuild.

Mother Theresa said "It's better to sweat in peace, than to bleed in war" and she was right.

You have been at war deep inside because it's likely that your natural instincts as a parent have been ignored. No blame. You did not know. No one talks about these things, yet.

There are things that you now know could have been done differently or should have had a different outcome. But all of that is past. Forgive, let go and exhale it out.

Today is all that exists, here and now and your presence in the moment.

> *"To attract joy and create more success, try doing less but doing it with more enthusiasm."*
>
> *- Phillip Humbert*

There is no do over in this life you've been given, there is just NOW and the world is in such a fragile state, we no longer even have the perceived security of a future anymore.

So what are you waiting for? Your children are there, waiting for you to step into that which is your destiny.

I know that they believe in you.

I believe in you.

The only question and my challenge to you is do *you* believe in you?

Begin.

14

EMPOWERING QUOTES

Use these quotes as I suggested, as sound bites of wisdom to recharge and refresh you. There is an abundance of wisdom in the words, and when you note the author of the quote, you will likely recognize the names (and lives) of greatness.

Carry this book and just flip open to a quote to put you back into perspective and to remind you that most of your behaviors towards your child are simply out of habit or observation of others' behaviors towards their children. I hate to say it but "money see, monkey do". Don't be a monkey.

> *"The illiterate of the 21st century will not be those who cannot read and write, but those who cannot learn, unlearn and relearn."*
>
> *- Alvin Toffler*

> *"You have to give them unconditional love. They need to know that even if they screw up, you love them. You don't want them to grow up and resent you or, even worse, parent the way you parented them."*
>
> *- Alfie Kohn*

> *"School is the advertising agency which makes you believe that you need the society as it is."*
>
> *Ivan Illich*

"Believe nothing merely because you have been told it . . . or because it is tradition, or because you yourselves have imagined it. Do not believe what your teacher tells you merely out of respect for the teacher. But whatsoever, after due examination and analysis, you find to be conductive to the good, the benefit, the welfare of all beings – that doctrine believe and cling to, and take it as your guide."

- Gautama Buddha

"Living is learning and when kids are living fully and energetically and happily they are learning a lot, even if we don't always know what it is."

- John Holt

In short, *"Do this and you'll get that"* makes people focus on the *"that"* not the *"this."* Do rewards motivate people? Absolutely. They motivate people to get rewards.

- Alfie Kohn

"Sometimes we have to put our foot down, ... but before we deliberately make children unhappy in order to get them to get into the car, or to do their homework or whatever, we need to weigh whether what we're doing to make it happen is worth the possible strain on our relationship with them."

- Alfie Kohn

"'The future is here. It's just not widely distributed yet."
- William Gibson

"We teachers - perhaps all human beings - are in the grip of an astonishing delusion. We think that we can take a picture, a structure, a working model of something, constructed in our minds out of long experience and familiarity, and by turning that model into a string of words, transplant it whole into the mind of someone else. Perhaps once in a thousand times, when

the explanation is extraordinary good, and the listener extraordinary experienced and skillful at turning word strings into non-verbal reality, and when the explainer and listener share in common many of the experiences being talked about, the process may work, and some real meaning may be communicated. Most of the time, explaining does not increase understanding, and may even lessen it."

- John Holt

"Everybody is a genius. But if you judge a fish by its ability to climb a tree, it will spend its whole life believing that it is stupid."

- Albert Einstein

"I think children need much more than they have of opportunities to come into contact with adults who are seriously doing their adult thing, not just hanging around entertaining or instructing or being nice to children. They also need much more than they have of opportunities to get away from adults altogether, and live their lives free of other people's anxious attention."

- John Holt

"The uncreative mind can spot wrong answers, but it takes a creative mind to spot a wrong question."

- Anthony Jay

"The child is curious. He wants to make sense out of things, find out how things work, gain competence and control over himself and his environment, and do what he can see other people doing. He is open, perceptive, and experimental. He does not merely observe the world around him, He does not shut himself off from the strange, complicated world around him, but tastes it, touches it, hefts it, bends it, breaks it. To find out how reality works, he works on it. He is bold. He is not afraid of making

mistakes. And he is patient. He can tolerate an extraordinary amount of uncertainty, confusion, ignorance, and suspense ... School is not a place that gives much time, or opportunity, or reward, for this kind of thinking and learning."

- John Holt

"All I am saying can be summed up in two words: Trust Children. Nothing could be simpler, or more difficult. Difficult because to trust children we must first learn to trust ourselves, and most of us were taught as children that we could not be trusted."

- John Holt

"The whole educational and professional training system is a very elaborate filter, which just weeds out people who are too independent, and who think for themselves, and who don't know how to be submissive, and so on – because they're dysfunctional to the institutions."

- Noam Chomsky

"Traditional education focuses on teaching, not learning. It incorrectly assumes that for every ounce of teaching there is an ounce of learning by those who are taught. However, most of what we learn before, during, and after attending schools is learned without its being taught to us. A child learns such fundamental things as how to walk, talk, eat, and dress, and so on without being taught these things. Adults learn most of what they use at work or at leisure while at work or leisure. Most of what is taught in classroom settings is forgotten, and much or what is remembered is irrelevant."

- Russell Ackoff

"Schools are designed on the assumption that there is a secret to everything in life; that the quality of life depends upon knowing that secret; that secrets can only be known in orderly succes-

sions; and that only teachers can properly reveal these secrets. An individual with a schooled mind conceives of the world as a pyramid of classified packages accessible only to those who carry the proper tags."

- Ivan Illich

"When test scores go up, we should worry, because of how poor a measure they are of what matters, and what you typically sacrifice in a desperate effort to raise scores."

- Alfie Kohn

"Nothing bothers me more than when people criticize my criticism of school by telling me that schools are not just places to learn math and spelling, they are places where children learn a vaguely defined thing called socialization. I know. I think schools generally do an effective and terribly damaging job of teaching children to be infantile, dependent, intellectually dishonest, passive and disrespectful to their own developmental capacities."

- Seymour Papert

"To develop a complete mind: study the science of art; study the art of science. Learn how to see. Realize that everything connects to everything else."

- Leonardo da Vinci

"Do not train children in learning by force and harshness, but direct them to it by what amuses their minds, so that you may be better able to discover with accuracy the peculiar bent of the genius of each."

- Plato

"What children need is not new and better curricula but access to more and more of the real world; plenty of time and space to think over their experiences, and to use fantasy and play to make

meaning out of them; and advice, road maps, guidebooks, to make it easier for them to get where they want to go (not where we think they ought to go), and to find out what they want to find out."

- John Holt

"We destroy the disinterested (I do not mean uninterested) love of learning in children, which is so strong when they are small, by encouraging and compelling them to work for petty and contemptible rewards — gold stars, or papers marked 100 and tacked to the wall, or A's on report cards... in short, for the ignoble satisfaction of feeling that they are better than someone else.... We kill, not only their curiosity, but their feeling that it is a good and admirable thing to be curious, so that by the age of ten most of them will not ask questions, and will show a good deal of scorn for the few who do."

- John Holt

"There is no neutral education. Education is either for domestication or for freedom."

- Joao Coutinho

"What is the purpose of industrial education? To fill the young of the species with knowledge and awaken their intelligence? Nothing could be further from the truth. The aim is simply to reduce as many individuals as possible to the same safe level, to breed and train a standardized citizenry, to put down dissent and originality. That is its aim in the United States and that is its aim everywhere else."

- H. L. Mencken

"Life can only be understood backwards but you have to live it forward. You can only do that by stepping into uncertainty and by trying, within this uncertainty, to create your own islands of security.... The new security will be a belief that ...if this

doesn't work out you could do something else. You are your own security."

- Charles Handy

"Because schools suffocate children's hunger to learn, learning appears to be difficult and we assume that children must be externally motivated to do it. As a society, we must own up to the damage we do to our children... in our families and in our schools. We must also be willing to make the sweeping changes in our institutions, public policies and personal lives that are necessary to reverse that harm to our children and to our society."

- Wendy Priesnitz

"In the end, the secret to learning is so simple: forget about it. Think only about whatever you love. Follow it, do it, dream about it. One day, you will glance up at your collection of Japanese literature, or trip over the solar oven you built, and it will hit you: learning was there all the time, happening by itself."

- Grace Llewellyn

"I've concluded that genius is as common as dirt. We suppress our genius only because we haven't yet figured out how to manage a population of educated men and women. The solution, I think, is simple and glorious. Let them manage themselves."

- John Taylor Gatto

"Public education reflects our society's paternalistic, hierarchical world view, which exploits children in the same way it takes the earth's resources for granted."

- Wendy Priesnitz

"I don't think we'll get rid of schools any time soon, certainly not in my lifetime, but if we're going to change what's rapidly becoming a disaster of ignorance, we need to realize that the

school institution "schools" very well, though it does not "educate"; that's inherent in the design of the thing. It's not the fault of bad teachers or too little money spent. It's just impossible for education and schooling ever to be the same thing."

- John Taylor Gatto

"It is as true now as it was then that no matter what tests show, very little of what is taught in school is learned, very little of what is learned is remembered, and very little of what is remembered is used. The things we learn, remember, and use are the things we seek out or meet in the daily, serious, non-school parts of our lives."

- John Holt

"... 'How will they learn to read?' you ask, and my answer is 'Remember the lessons of Massachusetts.' When children are given whole lives instead of age-graded ones in cell blocks, they learn to read, write, and do arithmetic with ease, if those things make sense in the kind of life that unfolds around them."

- John Taylor Gatto

"Our large schools are organized like a factory of the late 19th century: top down, command control management, a system designed to stifle creativity and independent judgment."

- David T Kearns

"I imagine a school system that recognizes learning is natural, that a love of learning is normal, and that real learning is passionate learning. A school curriculum that values questions above answers... creativity above fact regurgitation... individuality above conformity... and excellence above standardized performance..... And we must reject all notions of 'reform' that serve up more of the same: more testing, more 'standards', more uniformity, more conformity, and more bureaucracy."

- Tom Peter

"A child only pours herself into a little funnel or into a little box when she's afraid of the world - when she's been defeated. But when a child is doing something she's passionately interested in, she grows like a tree - in all directions. This is how children learn, how children grow. They send down a taproot like a tree in dry soil. The tree may be stunted, but it sends out these roots, and suddenly one of these little taproots goes down and strikes a source of water. And the whole tree grows."

- John Holt

"What is equally striking to me is this ... there isn't a sense of a community solving problems together, rather there's punishment for aberrant individuals."

- Alfie Kohn

"About reading, children learn something much more difficult than reading without instruction - namely, to speak and understand their native language. I do not think they would or could learn it if they were instructed. I think reading instruction is the enemy of reading."

- John Holt

"Just as eating contrary to the inclination is injurious to the health, so study without desire spoils the memory, and it retains nothing that it takes in."

- Leonardo da Vinci

"Education is what remains after one has forgotten everything he learned in school. It is a miracle that curiosity survives formal education."

- Albert Einstein

"The structure of American schooling, 20th century style, began in 1806 when Napoleon's amateur soldiers beat the professional soldiers of Prussia at the battle of Jena. When your

business is selling soldiers, losing a battle like that is serious. Almost immediately afterwards a German philosopher named Fichte delivered his famous 'Address to the German Nation' which became one of the most influential documents in modern history. In effect he told the Prussian people that the party was over, that the nation would have to shape up through a new Utopian institution of forced schooling in which everyone would learn to take orders. So the world got compulsion schooling at the end of a state bayonet for the first time in human history; modern forced schooling started in Prussia in 1819 with a clear vision of what centralized schools could deliver: Obedient soldiers to the army; Obedient workers to the mines; Well subordinated civil servants to government; Well subordinated clerks to industry. Citizens who thought alike about major issues."

- John Taylor Gatto

"School is a twelve-year jail sentence where bad habits are the only curriculum truly learned."

- John Taylor Gatto

"The function of high school, then, is not so much to communicate knowledge as to oblige children finally to accept the grading system as a measure of their inner excellence. And a function of the self-destructive process in American children is to make them willing to accept not their own, but a variety of other standards, like a grading system, for measuring themselves. It is thus apparent that the way American culture is now integrated it would fall apart if it did not engender feelings of inferiority and worthlessness."

- Jules Henry

"Every child is an artist. The problem is how to remain an artist once he grows up."

- Pablo Picasso

"Education itself is a putting off, a postponement; we are told to work hard to get good results. Why? So we can get a good job. What is a good job? One that pays well. Oh. And that's it? All this suffering, merely so that we can earn a lot of money, which, even if we manage it, will not solve our problems anyway? It's a tragically limited idea of what life is all about."

- Tom Hodgkinson

"Children do not need to be made to learn to be better, told what to do or shown how. If they are given access to enough of the world, they will see clearly enough what things are truly important to themselves and to others, and they will make for themselves a better path into that world than anyone else could make for them."

- John Holt

"The modern world is dangerous, confusing, not meant for children, not generally kind or welcoming to them. We have much to learn about how to make the world more accessible to them, and how to give them more freedom and competence in exploring it. But this as a very different thing from designing nice little curricula."

- John Holt

"Our rapidly moving, information-based society badly needs people who know how to find facts rather than memorize them, and who know how to cope with change in creative ways. You don't learn those things in school."

- Wendy Priesnitz

"Very few things are as dangerous as a bunch of incentive-driven individuals trying to play it safe."

- Alfie Kohn

"We ask children to do for most of a day what few adults are

able to do for even an hour. How many of us, attending, say, a lecture that doesn't interest us, can keep our minds from wandering? Hardly any."

- John Holt

"It's absurd and anti-life to be part of a system that compels you to sit in confinement with people of exactly the same age and social class. That system effectively cuts you off from the immense diversity of life and the synergy of variety; indeed it cuts you off from your own past and future, sealing you in a continuous present much the same way television does..."

- John Taylor Gatto

"Educating the masses was intended only to improve the relationship between the top and the bottom of society. Not for changing the nature of the relationship."

- John Ralston Paul

"Education is what remains after one has forgotten everything he learned in school."

- Albert Einstein

"Of course, a child may not know what he may need to know in ten years (who does?), but he knows, and much better than anyone else, what he wants and needs to know right now, what his mind is ready and hungry for. If we help him, or just allow him, to learn that, he will remember it, use it, and build on it. If we try to make him learn something else, that we think is more important, the chances are that he won't learn it, or will learn very little of it, that he will soon forget most of what he learned, and what is worst of all, will before long lose most of his appetite for learning anything."

- John Holt

"I've come to believe that genius is an exceedingly common

human quality, probably natural to most of us... I began to wonder, reluctantly, whether it was possible that being in school itself was what was dumbing them down. Was it possible I had been hired not to enlarge children's power, but to diminish it? That seemed crazy on the face of it, but slowly I began to realize that the bells and the confinement, the crazy sequences, the age-segregation, the lack of privacy, the constant surveillance, and all the rest of national curriculum of schooling were designed exactly as if someone had set out to *prevent* children from learning how to think and act, to coax them into addiction and dependent behavior."

- John Taylor Gatto

"It's important to distinguish well-conducted from poorly conducted research, and to understand the outcome variables in a given investigation. For example, if someone were to announce that studies have shown traditional classroom discipline techniques are 'effective,' our immediate response should be to ask, 'Effective at what? Promoting meaningful learning? Concern for others? Or merely eliciting short-term obedience?' Empirical findings can come from rigorously conducted scientific studies but still be of limited value; everything depends on the objectives that informed the research."

- Alfie Kohn

"The condition of alienation, of being asleep, of being unconscious, of being out of one's mind, is the condition of the normal man. Society highly values its normal man. It educates children to lose themselves and to become absurd, and thus to be normal."

- R.D. Laing

"Learning is not the product of teaching. Learning is the product of the activity of learners."

- John Holt

"If we taught babies to talk as most skills are taught in school, they would memorize lists of sounds in a predetermined order and practice them alone in a closet."

- Linda Darling-Hammond

"We think of ways that we can control them, whether it be with a spanking or a gold sticker or a parent constantly saying, 'Good job, good job, good job.'"

- Alfie Kohn

"Most parents want to know what they can do to make their children do as they're told."

- Alfie Kohn

"By preventing a free market in education, a handful of social engineers - backed by the industries that profit from compulsory schooling: teacher colleges, textbook publishers, materials suppliers, et al. - has ensured that most of our children will not have an education, even though they may be thoroughly schooled."

- John Taylor Gatto

"What can we surmise about the likelihood of someone's being caring and generous, loving and helpful, just from knowing that they are a believer? Virtually nothing, say psychologists, sociologists, and others who have studied that question for decade."

- Alfie Kohn

"Educators — like musicians, journalists, car makers, and bankers before them — won't know what hit them. But as sure as change is overtaking every other sector of society, it will overtake education — as well it should. Our cookie-cutter, one-pace-fits-all, test-focused system is not up to the task of teaching the creators of the new Googles. Call me a utopian but I imagine a new educational ecology where students may take courses from

*anywhere and instructors may select any students, where cours-
es are collaborative and public, where creativity is nurtured as
Google nurtures it, where making mistakes well is valued over
sameness and safety, where education continues long past age
21, where tests and degrees matter less than one's own portfolio
of work, where the gift economy may turn anyone with knowledge into teachers, where the skills of research and reasoning
and skepticism are valued over the skills of memorization and
calculation, and where universities teach an abundance of
knowledge to those who want it rather than manage a scarcity
of seats in a class."*

- Jeff Jarvis

*"You have to welcome their arguing with you, not to the point
of disrespect, but if they are going to stand up for themselves,
they need to learn to argue effectively,"*

- Alfie Kohn

*"Think of the things killing us as a nation: narcotic drugs,
brainless competition, dishonesty, greed, recreational sex, the
pornography of violence, gambling, alcohol, and — the worst
pornography of all — lives devoted to buying things, accumu-
lation as a philosophy. All of these are addictions of dependent
personalities. That is what our brand of schooling must inevi-
tably produce. A large fraction of our total economy has grown
up around providing service and counseling to inadequate people, and inadequate people are the main product of government
compulsion schools."*

- John Taylor Gatto

*"I am beginning to suspect all elaborate and special systems
of education. They seem to me to be built upon the supposition
that every child is a kind of idiot who must be taught to think.
Whereas, if the child is left to himself, he will think more and
better, if less showily. Let him go and come freely, let him touch*

real things and combine his impressions for himself, instead of sitting indoors at a little round table, while a sweet-voiced teacher suggests that he build a stone wall with his wooden blocks, or make a rainbow out of strips of colored paper, or plant straw trees in bead flower-pots. Such teaching fills the mind with artificial associations that must be got rid of, before the child can develop independent ideas out of actual experience."

- Anne Sullivan, Helen Keller's Teacher

"To live a creative life, we must lose our fear of being wrong."
- Joseph Chilton Pearce

"When we do things that are controlling, whether intentional or not, we are not going to get those long-term outcomes."
- Alfie Kohn

"Whatever an education is, it should make you a unique individual, not a conformist; it should furnish you with an original spirit with which to tackle the big challenges; it should allow you to find values which will be your road map through life; it should make you spiritually rich, a person who loves whatever you are doing, wherever you are, whomever you are with; it should teach you what is important, how to live and how to die."
- John Taylor Gatto

"We who believe that children want to learn about the world, are good at it, and can be trusted to do it with very little adult coercion or interference, are probably no more than one percent of the population, if that. And we are not likely to become the majority in my lifetime. This doesn't trouble me much anymore, as long as this minority keeps on growing. My work is to help it grow."
- John Holt

"I applaud Sudbury Valley's focus on freedom, but not what I take to be an inattention to community. Sudbury has a libertarian bent, and the world view seems to see all adult involvement as an authoritarian restriction of personal autonomy. Total autonomy is not developmentally appropriate. Kids need guidance and many of them need structure at the same time that they need the opportunity to learn how to make good decisions."

- Alfie Kohn

"I can't help noting that no cultures in the word that I have ever heard of make such a fuss about children's bedtimes, and no cultures have so many adults who find it so hard either to go to sleep or wake up. Could these social facts be connected? I strongly suspect they are."

- John Holt

"The anxiety children feel at constantly being tested, their fear of failure, punishment, and disgrace, severely reduces their ability both to perceive and to remember, and drives them away from the material being studied into strategies for fooling teachers into thinking they know what they really don't know."

- John Holt

"There is, it seems, more concern about whether children learn the mechanics of reading and writing than grow to love reading and writing; learn about democracy than have practice in democracy; hear about knowledge... rather than gain experience in personally constructing knowledge... see the world narrowly, simple and ordered, rather than broad complex and uncertain."

- Vitto Perrone

"There must be a way to educate young children so that the great human qualities that we know are in them may be developed. But we'll never do it as long as we are obsessed with tests. At faculty meetings we talk about how to reward the thinkers in

our classes. Who is kidding whom? No amount of rewards and satisfactions obtained in the small group thinking sessions will make up to Monica for what she felt today, faced by a final test that she knew she couldn't do and was going to fail."

- John Holt

"Pleasant experiences don't make up for painful ones. No child, once painfully burned, would agree to be burned again, however enticing the reward. For all our talk and good intentions, there is much more stick than carrot in school, and while this remains so, children are going to adopt a strategy aimed above all else at staying out of trouble. How can we foster a joyous, alert, wholehearted participation in life if we build all our schooling around the holiness of getting 'right answers'?"

- John Holt

"Curiosity has no important place in my work, only conformity."

- John Taylor Gatto

"I have used the words "home schooling" to describe the process by which children grow and learn in the world without going, or going very much, to schools, because those words are familiar and quickly understood. But in one very important sense they are misleading. What is most important and valuable about the home as a base for children's growth in the word is not that it is a better school than the schools but that it isn't a school at all."

- John Holt

"Play is the only way the highest intelligence of humankind can unfold."

- Joseph Chilton Pearce

"Our politics, religion, news, athletics, education and commerce have been transformed into congenial adjuncts of show busi-

ness, largely without protest or even much popular notice. The result is that we are a people on the verge of amusing ourselves to death."

- Neil Postman

"Your children are not your children, they are the sons and daughters of life's longing for itself. They come through you but not from you, and though they are with you yet they belong not to you. You may give them your love but not your thoughts, for they have their own thoughts. You may house their bodies but not their souls, for their souls dwell in the house of tomorrow, which you cannot visit, not even in your dreams. You may strive to be like them, but seek not to make them like you. For life goes not backward nor tarries with yesterday."

- Kahlil Gibran

"Whatever they grow up to be, they are still our children, and the one most important of all the things we can give to them is unconditional love. Not a love that depends on anything at all except that they are our children."

- Rosaleen Dickson

"Children are like wet cement. Whatever falls on them makes an impression."

- Dr. Haim Ginott

"Education consists mainly in what we have unlearned."
- Mark Twain

"We must accept that this creative pulse within us is God's creative pulse itself."

- Joseph Chilton Pearce

"Leaders are not, as we are often led to think, people who go along with huge crowds following them. Leaders are people who

go their own way without caring, or even looking to see, whether anyone is following them. "Leadership qualities" are not the qualities that enable people to attract followers, but those that enable them to do without them. They include, at the very least, courage, endurance, patience, humor, flexibility, resourcefulness, stubbornness, a keen sense of reality, and the ability to keep a cool and clear head, even when things are going badly. True leaders, in short, do not make people into followers, but into other leaders."

- John Holt

"You can discover more about a person in an hour of play than in a year of conversation."

- Plato

"Soap and education are not as sudden as a massacre, but they are more deadly in the long run."

- Mark Twain

"If we continually try to force a child to do what he is afraid to do, he will become more timid, and will use his brains and energy, not to explore the unknown, but to find ways to avoid the pressures we put on him."

- John Holt

"Let there be spaces in your togetherness, and let the winds of the heavens dance between you. Love one another but make not a bond of love: Let it rather be a moving sea between the shores of your souls. Fill each other's cup but drink not from one cup. Give one another of your bread but eat not from the same loaf. Sing and dance together and be joyous, but let each one of you be alone, Even as the strings of a lute are alone though they quiver with the same music. Give your hearts, but not into each other's keeping. For only the hand of Life can contain your hearts. And stand together, yet not too near together: For the pil-

lars of the temple stand apart, and the oak tree and the cypress grow not in each other's shadow."

- Kahlil Gibran

"In every real man a child is hidden that wants to play."

- Friedrich Nietzsche

"I remember that I was never able to get along at school. I was at the foot of the class."

- Thomas Edison

"Just play. Have fun. Enjoy the game."

- Michael Jordan

"No human relation gives one possession in another - every two souls are absolutely different. In friendship or in love, the two side by side raise hands together to find what one cannot reach alone."

- Kahlil Gibran

"Life must be lived as play."

- Plato

"It is paradoxical that many educators and parents still differentiate between a time for learning and a time for play without seeing the vital connection between them."

- Leo Buscaglia

"School is where you go between when your parents can't take you, and industry can't take you."

- John Updike

"What makes people smart, curious, alert, observant, competent, confident, resourceful, persistent - in the broadest and best sense, intelligent- is not having access to more and more learn-

ing places, resources, and specialists, but being able in their lives to do a wide variety of interesting things that matter, things that challenge their ingenuity, skill, and judgment, and that make an obvious difference in their lives and the lives of people around them."

- John Holt

"What does education often do? It makes a straight-cut ditch of a free, meandering brook."

- Henry David Thoreau

"What we call education and culture is for the most part nothing but the substitution of reading for experience, of literature for life, of the obsolete fictitious for the contemporary real."

- George Bernard Shaw

"Thank goodness I was never sent to school; it would have rubbed off some of the originality."

- Helen Beatrix Potter

"Since every effort in our educational life seems to be directed toward making of the child a being foreign to itself, it must of necessity produce individuals foreign to one another, and in everlasting antagonism with each other."

- Emma Goldman

"The best education consists in immunizing people against systematic attempts at education."

- Paul Karl Feyerabend

"The whole theory of modern education is radically unsound. Fortunately in England, at any rate, education produces no effect whatsoever. If it did, it would prove a serious danger to the upper classes, and probably lead to acts of violence."

- Oscar Wilde

"He was so learned that he could name a horse in nine languages; so ignorant that he bought a cow to ride on."

- Benjamin Franklin

"Examinations are formidable even to the best prepared, for the greatest fool may ask more than the wisest man can answer."

- C. C. Colton

"It is our American habit, if we find the foundations of our educational structure unsatisfactory, to add another story or a wing."

- John Dewey

"Much that passes for education is not education at all but ritual. The fact is that we are being educated when we know it least."

- David P. Gardner

"How I hated schools, and what a life of anxiety I lived there. I counted the hours to the end of every term, when I should return home."

- Winston Churchill

"Education is an admirable thing, but it is well to remember from time to time that nothing that is worth knowing can be taught."

- Oscar Wilde

"The average schoolmaster is and always must be essentially an ass, for how can one imagine an intelligent man engaging in so puerile an avocation."

- H. L. Mencken

"The trouble with being educated is that it takes a long time; it uses up the better part of your life and when you are finished

what you know is that you would have benefited more by going into banking."

- Phillip K. Dick

"The essence of childhood, of course, is play, which my friends and I did endlessly on streets that we reluctantly shared with traffic."

- Bill Cosby

"Children are the world's most valuable resource and its best hope for the future."

- John Fitzgerald Kennedy

"Children will not remember you for the material things you provided but for the feeling that you cherished them."

- Richard L. Evans

"We are so accustomed to this prescriptive style of education whereby the aims, purposes and goals are pre-established for the learners that we seldom question it. Nor do we question the assumptions that underlie, or the alternatives to, such practices. Adherents of a constructivist philosophy of learning would argue, amongst other issues, that learning is a far more individualized process. Many constructivists believe that learning is most effective when learners, through interaction with their world, appropriate and reconstruct knowledge and experiences that are meaningful to their own interpretations. According to this perspective, the goals, objectives, content and even the aims of learning are thus highly personalized and are largely determined by the learners themselves."

- Neil Postman

"Adults are always asking little kids what they want to be when they grow up because they're looking for ideas"

- Paula Poundstone

"I still get wildly enthusiastic about little things... I play with leaves. I skip down the street and run against the wind."
- Leo Buscaglia

"The will to win, the desire to succeed, the urge to reach your full potential... these are the keys that will unlock the door to personal excellence."
- Confucius

"I have never let my schooling interfere with my education."
- Mark Twain

"The child must know that he is a miracle, that since the beginning of the world there hasn't been, and until the end of the world there will not be, another child like him."
- Pablo Casals

"While we try to teach our children all about life, our children teach us what life is all about."
- Anonymous

"Every child born into the world is a new thought of God, an ever fresh and radiant possibility"
- Kate Douglas Wiggin

"I've come to the frightening conclusion that I am the decisive element in the classroom. It's my daily mood that makes the weather. As a teacher, I possess a tremendous power to make a child's life miserable or joyous. I can be a tool of torture or an instrument of inspiration. I can humiliate or humor, hurt or heal. In all situations, it is my response that decides whether a crisis will be escalated or de-escalated and a child humanized or de-humanized."
- Dr. Haim Ginott

"Children are the hands by which we take hold of heaven."
                              - Henry Ward Beecher

"The most effective kind of education is that a child should play amongst lovely things."
                                                    - Plato

"Let us put our minds together and see what life we can make for our children."
                                          - Sitting Bull

"Children have never been very good at listening to their elders, but they have never failed to imitate them."
                                - James Arthur Baldwin

"Loving a child doesn't mean giving in to all his whims; to love him is to bring out the best in him, to teach him to love what is difficult."
                                       - Nadia Boulanger

"You will always be your child's favorite toy."
                                          - Vicki Lansky

"We call a child's mind "small" simply by habit; perhaps it is larger than ours is, for it can take in almost anything without effort."
                                     - Christopher Morley

"If you want your children to improve, let them overhear the nice things you say about them to others."
                                        - Dr. Haim Ginott

15

KNOWERS

And finally some wisdom from Osho.....Truth is not separate from you; it is your innermost core. So you need not to learn it from somebody else. Then what's the function of the Masters?

The function of the Masters is to help you drop your knowledge, to help you unlearn, to help you towards a state of un-conditioning. Your knowledge means you will be always looking through a curtain and that curtain will distort everything. And knowledge is dead. Consciousness is needed, knowing is needed, a state of seeing is needed, but not knowledge. How can you know the alive through the dead?

A man stepped into a very crowded bus. After a while he took out his glass eye, threw it up in the air, and then put it back in again. Ten minutes later he again took out his glass eye, threw it up in the air, and then put it back in again.

The lady next to him was horrified. "What are you doing?" she cried. "I am just trying to see if there is any room up front."

That's what knowledge is: a glass eye.

You cannot see through it, it is impossible to see through it.

Drop all your conclusions -- Hindu, Christian, Mohammedan, Jaina, Jewish. Drop all the knowledge that has been forced upon you. Every child has been poisoned -- poisoned by knowledge, poisoned by the parents, the society, the church, the state.

Every child has been distracted from his innocence, from his not-knowing. And that's why every child, slowly, slowly, becomes so burdened that he loses all joy of life, all ecstasy of being, and he becomes just like the crowd, part of the crowd.

In fact, the moment a child is perfectly conditioned by you, you are very happy; you call it "religious education." You are very happy that the child has been initiated into the religion of his parents. All that you have done is you have destroyed his capacity to know on his own. You have destroyed his authenticity. You have destroyed his very precious innocence. You have closed his doors and windows.

Now he will live an encapsulated existence. He will live in his inner darkness, surrounded by all kinds of stupid theories, systems of thought, philosophies, and ideologies. He will be lost in a jungle of words and he will not be able to come out of it easily.

Even if he comes across a Master, if he meets a Buddha, then too it will take years for him to unlearn -- because learning becomes almost your blood, your bones, and your marrow. And to go against your own knowledge seems to be going against yourself, against your tradition, against your country, against your religion.

It seems as if you are a traitor, as if you are betraying. In fact, your society has betrayed you, has contaminated your soul.

Every society has been doing that up to now, and every society has been very successfully doing it.

That's why it is so rare to find a Buddha; it is so rare to escape from the traps the society puts all around the child. And the child is so unaware; he can easily be conditioned, hypnotized. And that's what goes on and on in the temples, in the churches, in the schools, colleges, universities. They all serve the past; they don't serve the future.

Their function is to perpetuate the past, the dead past. My work here is just the opposite. I am not here to perpetuate the past; hence I am against all knowledge.

I am all for learning, but learning means innocence, learning means openness, learning means receptivity. Learning means a non-egoistic approach towards reality. Learning means: "I don't know and I am ready -- ready to know."

Knowledge means: "I know already."

Knowledge is the greatest deception that society creates in people's minds.

My function is to serve the future, not the past. The past is no more, but the future is coming every moment. I want you to become innocent, seers, knowers -- not knowledgeable -- alert, aware, not unconsciously clinging to conclusions.

Welcome to the New Paradigm.

PRAISE

As an indie author, I want to let you know how important getting reviews is. First of all, it is a way you can communicate with me (and others who are looking at the book) and sharing your feedback and experience. I read every review and make notes to improve the newer and upcoming editions of my books. I also see if there is a specific theme or subject that many people discuss or mention, and that helps to inspire me to do further research and write more books.

Leaving a review on sites like Amazon.com also helps my author ranking on Amazon and therefore puts my books in front of more people who are searching for them.

If you feel this book has opened your mind, lit a fire in your belly or inspired you to action, then please take the few minutes it will take you to leave a review. Here is a handy link for you to do that now:

https://www.amazon.com/review/create-review?&asin=B00RCD85U0#

And below is a link to a "THANK YOU" video which I made especially for you, the reader. Just follow the link to watch the short video.

https://www.youtube.com/watch?v=KK8ti6L6hJU

Here are what some other people have said about this book...

The Natural Inquisitiveness of Children Should Be Encouraged.
March 29, 2013
By Monika

There were moments when I agreed with Hilmar-Jezek wholeheartedly. The natural inquisitiveness of children should be encouraged. They do have a powerful, innate desire to learn. Children need to be given opportunities to seek out deeper knowledge when a topic interests them, as well as the space to actually experience it. I loved when she wrote: "We have to understand and accept that learning is so much more than the acquisition of mass quantities of information. Education should strive to awaken the child's natural capabilities, and not educate.

A Must-Read for All Parents and Educators!
January 5, 2015
By Irina

This book is impossible to put down once you start reading it... As a homeschooling parent who has raised and homeschooled four children (with amazing results), I applaud Ms. Kytka Hilmar-Jezek's honest approach in educating the masses and exposing the dark reality of schools and the broken educational system. This book will strike chords. However, it will also make parents think twice before choosing career over raising their children and trusting the schools to do a parent's job. If more parents followed the advice of this book and actually parented their children, spent more time with them, became friends, and talked with their children, as opposed to leaving that task for the schools, while pursuing their own careers, we would have a much healthier society today. Bravo to the author for stating the facts so boldly

My Mind Has Been Opened to New Educational Possibilities...
March 28, 2013
By Yuliya (London)

This book opened my mind to a new way of thinking about my child's education. More importantly about them growing up in modern society. My child is smart, it's very easy to pass the responsibility on to others to educate and in most cases we are the first to complain when they fail. This book is about taking responsibility to educate your child so that he or she will be a more remarkable person and more importantly show you how to proceed with some inspirational ideas. I enjoyed and will certainly act on this information.

Interesting and informative book
December 20, 2014
By Stuart Powell

I love the message of this book. And it provides such great reminders. A must read for every parent and teacher, this book will change the way that you interact with children. This is a read-more-than-once book. Very inspiring and motivational. I think in time I will even have my children read it. Every homeschooler could learn a thing or two from this book.

One for every Unschooler's Shelf... In fact, every PARENT'S shelf.
We are all 'Born to Learn'
17 Dec 2014
By JL Morse

Oh how I wish I had found this gem at the start of our homeschooling adventure - for that matter, I would thoroughly recommend Kytka Hilmar-Jezek's Born to Learn to any parent; ones starting their journey into education, or those further along the line who feel there is 'something missing' in the way modern systems approach structured learning.

Jezek draws from the Unschooling/Home Education giants from John Taylor Gatto and John Holt to the Buddha, and presents a cohesive introduction to these thought leaders' views in an approachable and understandable way. Having raised three children in this paradigm, she introduces why a formal school environment might not be the best environment to raise entrepreneurs and free thinkers of our future generation.

Jezek has significant experience in the Waldorf/Steiner alternative education movement, which is also discussed to some lengths - yet unschooling as a philosophy is so much more than 'alternative' - It is a fundamental approach to how we view the nature and potential of our children, of humanity even - It is positive, brimming with potential, nurturing and loving - Rather than prescriptive, delineated and artificially constructed (such as mainstream educational establishments have become, if not designed to be). She presents a stimulating view of society where love is valued over fear, passion over prescription, dreamers and do-ers over naysayers and maintaining the 'status quo'...

I wholeheartedly recommend Born to Learn; it is full of inspirational quotes and anecdotes of free, passion-led learning and spiritual guidance, to inspire, supplement and support your journey into whole life learning (not just between the arbitrary ages of compulsory education; the term itself an anathema to the ongoing pursuit of human potential).

Beyond 5 Stars - Elegant Manifesto
& Wake-Up Call for New Parents
April 6, 2013
By Robert Steele

This slim but extremely coherent and pointed book goes into my best of the best list, 6 Stars, where the top 10% and especially gifted books go. Unschooling, the author makes clear, is not the same as homeschooling, and this may unnerve some, including those who are predisposed toward breaking away from the Prussian educational model intended to create obedient factory workers and soldiers rather than actually educate.

The author is acutely aware that neither homeschooling nor unschooling are remotely possible for most families as we approach the final collapse of a very corrupt economic system optimized to concentrate wealth for the 1% at the expense of the 99%. For this reason her ideas are best embraced as part of a total transformation that includes a return to a one-income family economy in which the family is placed ahead of all other considerations in every policy domain.

Having said that, while the author herself avoids specifics, this book is for me priceless at three levels:

LEVEL 1: At least understand the agony of your child in regimented schools. I have been serving as a substitute school teacher across Fairfax County, Virginia for the past month, every day, and while Fairfax is the "best of the best" in meticulously scheduled "teach to the test," the glaring deficiency I see everywhere is "intellectual free play." I've even had an assistant principal upset with me because I had the temerity to put the honors civics class desks in a circle -- an elementary principle had a problem with my mentioning Santa Clause, considered "an inappropriate religious reference" in the fine print. If nothing else -- and worth GOLD to any parent -- this book clearly establishes what we give up in sending our children into regimented public education (private schools teach 14 things public schools do not, look up John Taylor Gatto's 14 Principles of Elite Private Schools).

CAVEAT: What I am also seeing is that the kids are already smarter and more connected by our generation of adults, and many of them of them have already made the decision to tune out of rote learning and follow their own paths. If the schools do not start adapting soon, we will have more and more drop-outs, and it will be the best and the brightest dropping out, not the more challenged. School is not a challenge, it is a prison (in the view of many of its denizens).

LEVEL 2: Consider supplementing regime schooling with home schooling by at the very least taking steps to ensure your child has access to and learns how to leverage the vast range of truly extraordinary resources that are available online and through various networks including the Waldorf Homeschoolers, founded by the author.

LEVEL 3: Consider early on in the first pregnancy the relative merits of choosing to forgo the mother's earning potential for 18 years -- or even the first six. In our families case, my wife was able to work from 10 am to 2 pm Tue-Thu and was available to our children the rest of the time. The benefits for the first child were enormous, and cascaded down to the second and third.

There is only one truly radical statement in this book and I agree with it completely: the feminist movement that liberated women destroyed the family. Whether the feminist movement was part of an over-all campaign to further fragment the 99% and break up the middle class is for future historians to determine; what is absolutely clear is that by demeaning the role of the mother and the social and economic gains for any family and any society of mothers as home-makers, home-schoolers, and home-base, the feminist movement did for white women what prisons do for black fathers -- took them out. We all lost.

The language and presentation is as good as could be. This is not a lecturing, patronizing, or critical book as much as a sharing of perspective book. It makes an ideal gift for first-time parents. It makes an ideal gift for parents who have a child in school and are worried about the school telling them their child has attention deficit disorder -- it is the school that is out of order, not the child.

All told, a tremendous read that I also recommend to any adult who still has an open mind and would like to consider flushing our entire system down the toilet -- every institution in the West has been corrupted to the bone -- in the USA specifically, we are on the verge of a revolution that might or might not terminate the two-party tyranny that fronts from Wall Street and Texas oil interests.

Here are ten other books I recommend:

1. The Monk and the Riddle: The Art of Creating a Life While Making a Living
2. The Extreme Searcher's Internet Handbook: A Guide for the Serious Searcher
3. Weapons of Mass Instruction: A Schoolteacher's Journey Through the Dark World of Compulsory Schooling
4. Philosophy and the Social Problem: The Annotated Edition
5. The Lessons of History by Durant, Will published by Simon & Schuster Hardcover
6. Ideas and Integrities: A Spontaneous Autobiographical Disclosure
7. Homeland Earth : A Manifesto for the New Millennium (Advances in Systems Theory, Complexity and the Human Sciences)
8. Seven Complex Lessons in Education for the Future (Education on the Move)
9. Empowering Public Wisdom: A Practical Vision of Citizen-Led Politics (Manifesto Series)
10. God and Science: Coming Full Circle?

Best wishes to all,
Robert Steele
INTELLIGENCE for EARTH:
Clarity, Diversity, Integrity & Sustainability

`My belief is that the child comes to us perfect and complete.'
December 22, 2014
By Grady Harp
Amazon Hall of Fame Reviewer

Kytka Hilmar-Jezek

California author and writing coach Kytka Hilmar-Jezek was born in Prague but now is based in California when she is not traveling. She is the founder of Distinct Press where she helps other writers share their stories. She also writes and creates branding, marketing and promotional books for business people and entrepreneurs.

In this immensely readable book Kytka discusses the learning process, especially as demonstrated in the way children learn to learn. Her own technique with her three children is the attachment parenting style, or as she states.' my children were born at home, before it was popular. They were carried in a sling when mothers were running alongside with jogging strollers. They were raised on a 100% raw and living goods diet, which now is gaining popularity, but then was almost unheard of then. They were home schooled and unschooled. They grew up with no television, no Nintendo, no Disney, no competitive sports. They weren't told to color in the lines of their coloring books - they had no coloring books, until they made their own. Yet they love to read, play games and challenge their friends to be more.'

Her books pages are filled with (for some) controversial thoughts, but spend time with her thinking and perhaps you will begin to understand the current crisis in higher 'education' and the plethora of the new media influences on our youngsters. `The true objective of education is to inspire and it's to prepare the young to educate themselves throughout their lives. Home and Unschooled children are entrusted to find their own learning become creators, leaders and the game changers of society... They do this because they feel valuable, innovative, creative and have something intrinsic and of value to contribute - something that is not learned but formed from their own will, so it is uniquely their own. Schooling, on the other hand, is the imposition of intellectual content and facts upon the child - filling them with OUR outside info, entering all of our data. Children are not data banks....' `It is already there. It is a part of the package. The child is already full and complete. And we have continued to ignore this, thinking that we can somehow improve what is already a perfect system.' `A child exists in a growing physical form, manifesting. A child is a process, a process of growth - we all are actually, but it is more obvious in the size and shape of a child. Evolution does happen, but it moves slowly and on a rhythm of its own, and it cannot be hurried.'

Sound wisdom such as this jumps off every page. For a synopsis of the book read the Amazon page entry. For the knowledge and concept Kytka imparts, digest this book slowly.

Very helpful book!
December 19, 2014
By Tesa

I bought this book when we were first considering home educating our children. I was doing a browse and this one popped up - I am so glad it did! It was the first book on the subject that I read, and it answered all of my questions as well as a few more that hadn't occurred to me. I recommend this book to everyone I meet who is considering Home Ed, so thought it was about time I left a recommendation here as well.

If you're considering taking your child out of mainstream (school) education, read this! You honestly won't regret it.

Really good book - an eye opener!
March 28, 2013
By Joe P.

Wow, I wasn't expecting such a great read. I'm a web marketer and enjoy traveling and working abroad but would always but heads with my wife about travel because she's was programmed with the old mentality that kids need to be in school, while on my side I never believed in the old broken "but functional" system, This book educated both of us about new things that we hadn't even considered about home schooling. It opened up my wife's mind about the possibility of moving abroad and home schooling our 8 year old son.

Homeschooling? You need to read this book!
March 28, 2013
By Claude Whitacre

After reading this book, I think it would have been better if I home schooled my son.

The author brings up the value of play at an early age, and the benefits it brings out in later childhood.

The author explain the reasons that providing the conditions for learning are even more important than teaching by rote methods.

There is much more, but I don't want to spoil it for you. Read the book, it's a fast read and discover for yourself how learning can really take place.

A Must Read For ALL Parents
March 28, 2013
By Scott Hoffman

As a parent, I am often conflicted by what my parenting "heart" tells me and what society and convention tells me. Kytka's book was a tremendous reminder to all parents to focus on the "heart" messages. While I don't believe that a parent should create an unlimited environment for their child, expanding the "fences" and allowing children to do what they do best is a strategy that will reduce stress and allow a child to find their way to places far beyond their reach if confined to traditional learning.

Even as I understand that schools have to be able to "commoditize" education on a large scale, my hope is that they will use Kytka's thoughts as a guiding force where EVERY child is valuable, not because of what they do, but because of who they are and I am thankful that Kytka chose to share this book with all parents.

Embrace Self-Growth, Productivity, Happiness, Wellness and Real Entrepreneurship. Amazing book!!!!
December 22, 2014
By Marta M.

Wow, what can I say! Hold on, I know what to say- LIFE-STYLE DESIGN, or, the art of lifestyle design.

I will first start off with my story (mini rant) and then relate to this book, OK? It's all interconnected. To be honest, when I was a kid, I dreaded going to school, even though I was a good student. Even when I was like 8, I would say to my parents that school is a waste of time, as I can absorb the same knowledge at home in less than half an hour and be more productive, play sports and learn new things. Unfortunately, this was, and probably still is illegal in Poland, where I am from, and my parents were working so I had to go somewhere, right? Yes, I am an entrepreneur, and most schools teach the opposite - how to become a slave of the system (of course, there is nothing wrong with working for someone else, I am not a hardcore lifestyle designer- "work from home" as the only way).

What the school gave me was nervousness, anxiety, insomnia, lack of appetite and poor immune system. University was also sort of useless, luckily it's free in Poland. I quite enjoyed high school as the one I went to, had a different (pretty experimental) teaching system that would teach responsibility and individualism and it allowed me to focus on my passion – languages - at master German and English in 2 years.

To sum up - the main benefit I got from schooling was to meet other kids, but my friendships would not last that long as again, I have always been a bit different and would spend my time on creative activities while other kids were mainstream. As

141

a teen I tried to adapt and follow the mainstream, but it did not pay off and this is how I learned to follow my intuition and be myself.

Now, with this rant out of the way - I would like to focus on the book as this is why the review section is for. You may be thinking that this is some natural new-age B.S., but it's not.

Look at the results. Kytka's son, wrote his first book when he was 10. Yes - 10. I have read and reviewed this book a few days ago. (*My Journey To Becoming a Mayan Shaman*) Her kids have so many different skills, that they can proudly call themselves entrepreneurs. They have lived (not only travelled to) in different countries. They probably know more than most of CEO's that the world has seen. They will never go broke or get stressed out.

Kytka herself is a self-educated woman. Her credentials speak for themselves and she continues to study and grow. She is both a naturopath - she studied the human body and a NLP practitioner - she also studied the human mind. Add to it Reiki master degree (the spirit part, right) She is not just some stay at home the latest herbal fad or Paleo wellness mommy (excuse my rant again) posing as an alternative expert, but the REAL deal. Just check out her BIO.

Funny thing - I have been talking about this concept of self-schooling with 2 good friends of mine and I will add it here as it relates to the gist of the book:

1. My friend who is a school teacher. She loves her job and is passionate about educating kids and she sees herself as a quite alternative person and she says that the concept of home schooling (aside from the fact that unfortunately it's illegal here in Spain where I live) makes kids anti-social. She believes in going to school every day. Then college and then get a job (work 8 hrs. a day and earn 1000 Euros a month - this is Spanish dream) yet then, she struggles to pay the bills, as the Spanish economic crisis stakes its toll on the education sector, and wonders how I do it that I can work from home, earn 3 times more that she does and have much more free time for my passions. Now, I am

not ready to have kids, but when I do, I am surely leaving Spain and my partner is sure about it too. (He's Spanish). We would never send our kids to a Spanish school, unless it's something like an international, alternative one. However, since we both work from home, what would be the point?

2. A good friend of mine who is into lifestyle design himself and working from home - he also criticizes the concept that Kytka presents (he did not even read this book), yet he does not see that he is almost 30 and spends 15 hours a day stuck in his home office, trying to work on his "passive income business model" while kids like Kytka's kids, have achieved much, much more than he has (even though they are teens) and they can relax and spend their 20's learning new skills and traveling the world. They write books and speak languages. Do you see my point here?

To sum up:

- Great book and I resonated with this author
- The book is not for everyone. Now, I am not saying that those who don't like it are dummies - I know that not everyone can work from home (what about doctors, policemen, firemen?) and what they do is really needed. However, I believe in an alternative schooling system that is inspired by home schooling and encourages creativity, passion, intuition, and real life experience.
- Some people choose home schooling but are not as smart and well-prepared as Kytka (not offending anyone), and so they are ready for disaster - and press, TV and nay-sayers are just waiting for those disasters to put people off home schooling...

10 STARS FOR THIS BOOK. IF KYTKA AND HER FAMILY ARE EVER IN MY NEIGHBORHOOD, I WOULD LOVE TO INVITE THEM OVER FOR LUNCH!

(**Note:** My daughter Zanna also wrote when she was 12 entitled *How To Get What Your Want for Girls* and my other daughter Zynnia wrote *How To Do Crowdfunding* when she was 10 years old. I'd love it if you checked them out!)

This Author Is At The Top Of Her Game - A Terrific Read!
March 28, 2013
By Darryl E. J. Ruff

My kids are now adults with families of their own. But when they were pre-school children, and had my wife and had I known what Dr. Kytka teaches in this book, we would have strongly considered homeschooling. This well-travelled Author is one of those rare intellects who spells out, in finite detail, why she chose to become an un-schooling parent to her 3 children. While Dr. Kytka has authored several books, her 19-year old son also writes books. Talk about a "chip off the old block" (although the Author is female and not really an "old block"!). A great read and highly recommended.

Opens Up New Possibilities
December 21, 2014
By Jeffrey

The author has explained how old models for education are rapidly becoming less relevant in today's society. She discusses how some of the old ways of teaching actually slow down the process.

She opens our eyes to the astonishing efficiency with which children learn so many things. With an open mind which is alert to the changing needs and the boundless curiosity of the child you can foster a child's love of learning by recognizing when it is best to get out of the way. At the end of the day it makes you think and it's definitely worth the read.

Alternatives to Schools for Children

April 2, 2013
By Linda Quotes

The author has a lot of experience of bringing her children up out of the school system, and she shares an alternative way of life which encourages their individual development. Statistics are included like 21 prisons were built in 10 years in California, with funding increased by 209%, whilst only one university was built, with only a 15% increase in funding.

These priorities don't make sense, and as long as nothing changes prisons will continue to fill up with the children who are being failed by schools. The author includes some interesting quotes too.

Power To The Children
December 31, 2014
By Remo Williams

Kytka Hilmar-Jezek's book struck a chord with me: as someone involved in the American system of education for the past 26 years as a substitute and as an aide, I know first-hand how broken the system is and how children need to be weaned from it to be un-schooled and properly educated. Being shut in a prison-like environment for eight hours a day, five days a week, told what to do, when to do it, and how to do it can break a young person's spirit and initiative. Any talk of "think for yourself" or "walk to the beat of a different drummer" is just hogwash. The children are brainwashed to know only what the establishment wants them to know and have the illusion that they have accessed knowledge.

The school system is presently trying to keep the children in school for longer hours and start them younger, under the pretext that they can't compete "out there." The answer is not more, but less. When I went to school in the '50s, I had only four hours of school a day (private French school) and I received the best education imaginable. To echo the late Murray Rothbard, education should be left to the private sector. Free enterprise will make sure things are run efficiently. Free enterprise, what a concept!

Children should be encouraged to find out for themselves; they should be encouraged to figure things out for themselves. They are inquisitive enough. Once they are on the true path of knowledge, they will thirst for truth. And then, watch out. The truth will set them free. And dangerous.

The Love of Learning Is An Amazing Gift!
January 7, 2015
By Richard and Liz
TOP 1000 REVIEWER

Mother of three, author Kytka has educated each one of her children at home. All three are talented in many ways, each is able to adapt from the poorest to the most affluent of lifestyles, now own their own businesses along with having a variety of survival and self-sufficiency skills.

Does the above sound like the kind of child you would like to raise? You can! Are you wondering if public school is really the best place for your child? Maybe your child is already struggling and you are not sure how to help? As the author says, "To allow the opening for a new reality, you must be willing to question the current reality." This can be devastating for some. As a reader as well as an avid home educator I fully sympathize as I did not always think the way I do now. Just as Kytka admits she has relaxed in her schooling style over the years, I admit to thinking that homeschooling was definitely NOT the way to go way back when but it took desperation and a definite change of heart to show me I was wrong and since our decision to educate our children ourselves we have never looked back. It is our choice as to the kind of parent we want to be! WOW! That sounds like a burden but it does not have to be. How do you see obstacles in life? As a problem or a challenge?

Kytka admits that her kids found it hard to converse with school kids their age because they (her kids) were not interested in the latest fashions or the newest video game. I have seen this with our children too. They can however converse with all ages about the "real" things of life.

Is traditional school a prison for children? It is important to note that the author does not expect you to just take her word for everything she says. She encourages to read a variety of different books so that you make an educated choice for yourself. The author is not against all schooling, she is FOR LEARNING and there is a difference. "Today's public school system is set up and designed against learning." What are the seven hidden lessons that American public schools teach? When did the family break down? Erin Pizzey wrote "Destroy the family and you destroy the country." Requiring kids to start school earlier and spend a greater length of time there will not solve the problem in today's educational system.

SO is unschooling your child all about letting them do exactly what they want whilst you, as the parent, spend your days sat in front of the TV watching soap operas? No! It is your job to provide stimulation - library, museums etc. You are to guide and teach them when required. Encourage your child to talk to people and ask questions. Set the example. Many times that will mean learning right alongside them. Encourage that natural love of learning that is already within them. Who do you think needs the most help? It's not the children!

Are you doing too much for your child? Do you need to get out of the way and let them learn? (I have heard so many complaints from parents who have children with special needs saying that their teachers in school do not challenge them enough but we need to be careful at home that do not fall into the same trap.) The world is changing. Let your child change and be ready.

This is a well-written and hard to dispute book. It is the author's testimony of how she has raised her three children and it has worked. The author also provides a lot of quotes and book suggestions not to mention, that unless you have your head in the sand, you can see many of the problems that she talks about in today's public schools. SO what didn't I like? In one chapter she talks about the "prefect child". I see where the author is coming from in that each of us is created uniquely but the author says that each child is perfect. I have to disagree here. I think "perfect" is a poor choice of word as no matter who we are, none of us is perfect. Yes, we were all created to be as we are but we still have faults and if we bring up our children to think they are perfect and can never do any wrong then we are likely to raise a spoiled brat.

I would and do recommend this book to anyone thinking of homeschooling their child. In everything there needs to be balance. Just like me, you may not agree with everything in this book but it will get you thinking. Remember, we are not cookie cutter people i.e. all the same. We all live in different environments and have varying talents. The main message of this book is to not dampen that naturally inquisitive spirit in your child. Let them choose what they want to study this week. Run with it! Be encouraged. You'll soon discover that they will learn far more than if you sat them down with a rigid curriculum. LOVE TO LEARN, you'll never regret it!

Just so you know, I was given a copy of this book in return for my honest review. The opinion expressed above is totally my own. I have no affiliation with the author at all.

Alternatives to Schools for Children
January 2, 2015
By Amazon Customer

Certainly a very fascinating book on learning and teaching children. Having kids of my own so it makes a lot of sense. Children are certainly born to learn and we need to tap that ability. Interesting, recommend to all parents, researchers and teachers.

RECOMMENDED READING

There are a few voices who have been advocating childhood, how children learn, child freedom and the problems with education that are really worth your time to locate and read. I suggest the first three books as an overview of HUMAN behavior as a prerequisite to learning more because I believe if you understand the nature of humans, you will better be able to absorb the following authors and their information.

> *The Continuum Concept* by Jean Liedloff
> *Original Wisdom: Stories of an Ancient Way of Knowing* by Robert Wolff
> *Power vs. Force: The Hidden Determinants of Human Behavior* by David R. Hawkins

John Taylor Gatto

> *The Underground History of American Education* by John Taylor Gatto
> *Dumbing Us Down: The Hidden Curriculum of Compulsory Schooling* by John Taylor Gatto and Thomas Moore
> *The Exhausted School: Bending the Bars of Traditional Education* by John Taylor Gatto
> *Weapons of Mass Instruction: A Schoolteacher's Journey through the Dark World of Compulsory Schooling* by John

Kytka Hilmar-Jezek

Taylor Gatto
A Different Kind of Teacher: Solving the Crisis of American Schooling by John Taylor Gatto

John Holt

How Children Learn by John Holt
How Children Fail by John Holt
Learning All the Time by John Holt
Instead of Education: Ways to Help People Do Things Better by John Holt
Escape From Childhood: The Needs and Rights of Children by John Holt

David Elkind

The Hurried Child: Growing Up Too Fast Too Soon - 25th Anniversary Edition by David Elkind
The Power of Play: Learning What Comes Naturally by David Elkind
All Grown Up and No Place to Go: Teenagers in Crisis, Revised Edition by David Elkind
Parenting on the Go: Birth to Six, A to Z by David Elkind
Miseducation: PRESCHOOLERS AT RISK by David Elkind
Ties That Stress: The New Family Imbalance by David Elkind
A Sympathetic Understanding of the Child: Birth to Sixteen (3rd Edition) by David Elkind
Children and Adolescents by David Elkind
Parenting Your Teenager by David Elkind
Images of the Young Child: Collected Essays on Development and Education by David Elkind
Child's Reality: Three Developmental Themes (John M. MacEachran Memorial Lecture Series) by David Elkind

Grandparenting: Understanding today's children by David Elkind

Development of the Child by David Elkind and Irving B. Weiner

Understanding Your Child from Birth to Sixteen by David Elkind

The Child and Society by David Elkind

Child Development and Education: Piagetian Perspective by David Elkind

Child Development: A Core Approach by Irving B. Weiner and David Elkind

Ivan Illich

Deschooling Society by Ivan Illich

Imprisoned in the Global Classroom by Ivan D. Illich

ABC: The Alphabetization of the Popular Mind by Ivan Illich and Barry Sanders

Neil Postman

The Disappearance of Childhood by Neil Postman

The End of Education: Redefining the Value of School by Neil Postman

Teaching as a Subversive Activity by Neil Postman and Charles Weingartner

Building a Bridge to the 18th Century: How the Past Can Improve Our Future by Neil Postman

Amusing Ourselves to Death: Public Discourse in the Age of Show Business by Neil Postman and Andrew Postman

Technopoly: The Surrender of Culture to Technology by Neil Postman

Conscientious Objections: Stirring Up Trouble about Language, Technology and Education by Neil Postman

Linguistics: A Revolution in Teaching by Neil Postman and

Charles Weingartner
Teaching As a Conserving Activity by Neil Postman
The Soft Revolution: A Student Handbook for Turning Schools around by Neil Postman and Charles Weingartner

Paul Goodman

Growing Up Absurd: Problems of Youth in the Organized Society by Paul Goodman and Casey Nelson Blake
Compulsory Mis-Education and the Community of Scholars by Paul Goodman
Growing Up Absurd: Problems of Youth in the Organized System by Paul Goodman
Parents' Day by Paul Goodman

Alfie Kohn

Unconditional Parenting: Moving from Rewards and Punishments to Love and Reason by Alfie Kohn
Punished by Rewards: The Trouble with Gold Stars, Incentive Plans, A's, Praise, and Other Bribes by Alfie Kohn
More Than a Score: The New Uprising against High-Stakes Testing by Jesse Hagopian, Alfie Kohn and Diane Ravitch
Beyond Discipline: From Compliance to Community by Alfie Kohn
The Homework Myth: Why Our Kids Get Too Much of a Bad Thing by Alfie Kohn
Feel-Bad Education: And Other Contrarian Essays on Children and Schooling by Alfie Kohn
No Contest: The Case against Competition by Alfie Kohn
The Schools Our Children Deserve: Moving Beyond Traditional Classrooms and "Tougher Standards" by Alfie Kohn
What does it mean to Be Well Educated? And Other Essays on Standards, Grading, and Other Follies by Alfie Kohn

The Case against Standardized Testing: Raising the Scores, Ruining the Schools by Alfie Kohn and Lois Bridges

Joseph Chilton Pearce

Magical Child by Joseph Chilton Pearce
Magical Parent Magical Child: The Art of Joyful Parenting by Michael Mendizza and Joseph Chilton Pearce
Evolution's End by Joseph C. Pearce
From Magical Child to Magical Teen: A Guide to Adolescent Development by Joseph Chilton Pearce
Magical Child Matures by Joseph Chilton Pearce

William Sears

The Successful Child: What Parents Can Do to Help Kids Turn Out Well by William Sears
The Discipline Book: How to Have a Better-Behaved Child from Birth to Age Ten by William and Martha Sears

Additional Reading

Adventure - The Value of Risk in Children's Play by Joan Almon
Ten Ways to Destroy the Imagination of Your Child by Mr. Anthony Esolen
Life under Compulsion: Ten Ways to Destroy the Humanity of Your Child by Mr. Anthony Esolen
The Teenage Liberation Handbook: How to Quit School and Get a Real Life and Education by Grace Llewellyn
You Are Your Child's First Teacher, Third Edition: Encouraging Your Child's Natural Development from Birth to Age Six by Rahima Baldwin Dancy
Free to Learn: Why Unleashing the Instinct to Play Will Make Our Children Happier, More Self-Reliant, and Better

Students for Life by Peter Gray

Wounded by School: Recapturing the Joy in Learning and Standing Up to Old School Culture by Kirsten Olson

Healing Stories for Challenging Behaviour by Susan Perrow

Free at Last: The Sudbury Valley School by Daniel Greenberg

The Cult of Common Core: Obama's Final Solution for Your Child's Mind and Our Country's Exceptionalism by Brad McQueen

Conform: Exposing the Truth about Common Core and Public Education by Glenn Beck

Too Cool For School: Schools do NOT Breed Intelligence - Why You Shouldn't Pursue Higher Education, College or University by Philos Sopher

Childhood and Emotion: Across Cultures 1450-1800 by Claudia Jarzebowski and Thomas Max Safley

ABOUT THE AUTHOR

Kytka Hilmar-Jezek has been involved in Waldorf Education since 1990. She holds a Doctorate in Naturopathy & is a Certified Childbirth Educator. In the late 1990's she was the owner of Hedgehog Farms catalog and later Enchanted Fairy Dreams, an on line store, both of which specialized in Waldorf-Inspired toys and books.

Kytka has written on the subjects of Waldorf Education, home birth, natural health, extended vaccination, circumcision, breastfeeding, attachment parenting, the family bed, and everything else that she considers "common sense parenting" for over 22 years. She sat as Advisory & Trustee at Three Cedars Waldorf School as well as leading the parent toddler group. She is the author of over twenty books on healing, family and education and is a #1 Bestselling Amazon author numerous times over.

She founded Waldorf Homeschoolers and W.I.S.H. (Waldorf Inspired Students at Home). She also founded the Waldorf Homeschoolers Yahoo Group, which at one time had over 22,000 active members in the community. (*This group no longer exists.*) She graduated her children from Waldorf-inspired home schooling to full time unschooling, allowing them to choose when, how, what and why they wish to learn. In the last 22 years, she has raised three awesome people who are all very active in similar initiatives in their own right.

Kytka Hilmar-Jezek

Kytka is a sought after speaker whose speaking style is real, raw and relevant to the pressing issues of today. Her approachable personality tends to have people "perceive her more as a Luminary than just a Leader, because she tends to light the path for others by being a living example of the subject matter she speaks about."

As they say, "the proof is in the pudding" and you only need spend a few moments with her family to see that what she advocates and practices, works!

Awards

>   Education Revolution Hall of Fame
>   Presidential Awards for Volunteering
>   Presidential Awards for Community Service

Diplomas & Certifications

>   Doctor of Naturopathy
>   Clinical Hypnotheray and Psychotherapy
>   Certification of Complete Mind Therapy
>   NLP Advanced Master Practitioner
>   Noesiterapy
>   Hypnotic Pain Control
>   Rapid Results Pain Consultant
>   Master Training in Neuro Linguistic Programming
>   Certified Practitioner of Time Empowerment
>   Certified Childbirth Educator
>   Reiki Master
>   Usui Shiki Ryoho Reiki Practitioner
>   Reverend
>   Minister
>   Spiritual Counselor
>   PhD in Religion
>   Missionary Doctor
>   Honorary Shaman
>   Bestselling Author
>   Greatest Accomplishment: Mom

Extremely passionate about teaching those around her to build a better 'self' through awareness of the power of possibility, Kytka uses her personal life experiences to foster paradigm shifts in the lives of those around her.

Her latest venture is a publishing company and she regularly works with young authors as well as the elderly to share their stories in the form of books, both kindle and traditional paper/hardback.

She welcomes contact from all new authors and asks that you submit your ideas and interest through the following:

www.DistinctPress.com/Get-Published

She is an award winning speaker and trainer, a seven time Amazon bestselling author, an entrepreneur and her children (*and best of friends*) are thoroughly convinced that she is in fact, Supermom.

Connect with Kytka through her publishing company, Distinct Press.

www.DistinctPress.com

Kytka speaks internationally on the subjects she has experienced and lived the past 25+ years. To contact Kytka for a speaking or interview opportunity, please direct inquiries to the following:

Kytka@DistinctPress.com

If you enjoyed this book - we would LOVE for you to *leave a review* in order to assist other parents on their journey by sharing your insights. Locate other books authored by Kytka:

http://www.amazon.com/Kytka-Hilmar-Jezek/e/B004LY-9WFK/

Kytka Hilmar-Jezek

Finally, we wish to express our gratitude for your purchase of this book and we hope that sharing our lives with you in this way inspires you with courage, strength and passion on your own parenting path.

CPSIA information can be obtained at www.ICGtesting.com
Printed in the USA
LVOW07s0418161215

466799LV00004B/217/P